T0078430

DERAILING DISAPPOINTMENT

APRIL PACKER

authorHOUSE®

AuthorHouse™
1663 Liberty Drive
Bloomington, IN 47403
www.authorhouse.com
Phone: 833-262-8899

Published by AuthorHouse 01/22/2021

ISBN: 978-1-6655-1454-5 (sc)
ISBN: 978-1-6655-1453-8 (e)

Contents

Foreword

Trouble is trouble. Period. When we feel like we're stuck in a world of trouble, we need an answer, a strategy, a way out, a fresh mind-set. We need a way of thinking that allows us to refocus our thoughts and put things in perspective. We don't need feel-good moments; we need fill-me-with-good moments. We need moments that empower us to slowly straighten our backs and lift our heads.

Derailing Disappointment will help you embrace the dirt on your face, pick your dusty, dirty self up off the ground, and send you walking down the road to your next stop on the journey of becoming the you *you* were intended to be. It's real, it's relevant, and it's relatable. Whether you are male or female—black, white, blue, or green—if you've got breath in your body and struggles to overcome, this is for you.

This book is an open casket of the things she's let die and a growing garden of the seeds she's planted to let live. It's an intimate look at her inner workings. It's an up-close look at how she *chooses* to be faith-filled and God-conscious in the "yuck" and the "yay!" of life. This is not a "Look at me, I'm happy all the time" book. It's a "Look at me, I've got junk to deal with, but I won't let it work a deal on me" book.

April is a longtime friend of mine. We've taught middle school together, served in women's ministry together, had coffee together, and just done plain, old life together. She's great to laugh with, cry with, talk strategy with, and be silly with too. All of those sentiments come alive in the pages of this book.

In each ridiculously funny story, April leaves us with a few good old-fashioned belly laughs. In each painstaking story, she leaves us feeling hopeful. Go on that journey with her. Feel the tears she's cried, feel the pain she's endured, and feel the joy that's colored her existence. Feel it and relate it to back to you. It's what I've let it do for me, and it's been transformational—even after thirty years of Christianity. I'm telling you, if you really take an introspective look at yourself as you read, you'll be free to walk out your victory. You will fall down, you will stumble, and you might even wrestle with yourself along the way, but that's okay. You'll be ready to *Derail Disappointment* each time it tries to derail you. Come on. Jump in. Take the dive. Let's go.

—Dr. Shelley Connell, EdD

Preface

I have struggled mightily while trying to finish this book. I have written and deleted. I have thought and rethought. I have experienced deep inner struggles in the process of deciding to write or not write. Mostly, I have felt that no one really wants to hear what I have to say. The enemy has tricked my mind and stunned my faith in this process. I stumbled, but I got back up. I experienced anger and self-pity, but I found the strength to keep fighting. I experienced despondency and despair, yet God met me at the point of my need.

This is a piece of my story. During the writing, I doubted who it might or might not help, it has helped me—first and foremost. I know that the changes in my life will always start with me and not with others. Since I have been elevated mentally, physically, and spiritually during this process, I have a strong belief that you will be blessed in some small measure by the words beyond this preface.

Some of the things you will read about will be a little surprising, but they are all true. I only want to share the truth of what I know and have experienced. I am not an expert, and I am not perfect at anything. However, I am a lifelong learner. I yearn to learn daily. The more I learn, the more I can become an asset for myself and for others. I don't mind sharing the yuck of my struggles if others are going to be motivated and inspired to move forward in their lives. My deepest desire is to see us all live our best lives!

I want to let you know that you are not alone in any situation. The enemy of our souls has fed us that lie for many generations. You are not alone in your situation. You do not have to fear or hide from the big bad wolf in your life. God's presence is greater than any battle you could ever face. In the chapters ahead, I present a few ways to employ your tools given in the Word of God.

I hope you will experience a change in your life. A great pastor I know and respect says, "If nothing changes, nothing changes." Now that is something to think about. I am very confident that change brings about a change. It doesn't matter how small or how big; change affects its surroundings. Thank you, Pastor Ricky, for that great insight!

As you read these pages, I pray for healthy changes in your life and a safe place to let go of everything holding you captive. Gather a few friends and have a conversation. Write more in your journal and discover more about yourself. Divinely connect and powerfully conquer as you discover God's presence and realness in your life. He has wonderful plans for your life and desires to show you how much He loves you if you only believe and receive.

Buckle up! Find your favorite reading spot! Get your reading glasses, which I have to do, and let's begin this journey. Remember that I am with you on every page.

Chapter 1

Just Thinking

Star light, star bright,

The first star I see tonight;

I wish I may, I wish I might,

Have the wish I wish tonight.

—Anonymous

Have you ever had a dream or a desire that you felt would never come true? Have you been praying to God to answer your prayers and give you the desires of your heart? Have you done what you feel is all that He has required in the Word—serve, seek, and honor Him— while waiting for those desires of your heart to come to pass? Many of us have, but we also noticed that day after day, week after week, month after month, and even year after year, nothing changes. These are the times when our faith is shaken and rocked to its core.

How many times have I asked why, sat up, cried at night, and struggled to fight the tears back during the day? Many of you are wondering what I have often wondered: Why do bad things happen to good people? Why am I stuck in this place of nothingness? Will God ever answer my prayers—or am I one of the forgotten ones? God is sovereign in all He does. Our finite wisdom cannot fully understand His ways or methods of bringing us to our best.

The hardest places in our lives inadvertently bring out the best in us and cause us to realize we are absolutely nothing without Christ and His awesome power:

> And He *changes* the times and the
> seasons; He removes kings and raises
> up kings; He gives wisdom to the wise

and knowledge to those who have understanding. (Daniel 2:21 NKJV; emphasis added).

God is the only One with power and authority to cause change in our lives. Yes, there are things we can do to help the process, but promotions come from Him in every area of our lives. We will trust Him to move on our behalf. Change is inevitable in our lives when we choose to grow in Christ.

God is powerful and is able to sway or blow the wind how He chooses. We have been given free will to make choices in our lives. It is my prayer that my choices are pleasing to Him and that they are what He is leading me to do. Like many of you, I desperately want to see changes in my life, yet I am unsure of how to get there at times! I pray, I fast, and I live to the very best of my ability, yet my desires are seemingly visible but out of reach.

God, help! I need you! It is very hard to see others

progress around you—not that you want what others have. Again, I ask myself and God, *How do I get there? Will my life be filled with desires that are never going to be fulfilled? Why do I get up in the mornings? Why do I try?* Many days, my life has been zapped of zest. *Will I ever have my own family to love and cherish and honor You with, Abba? Will I ever be able to shop for the things I want instead of always sticking to a needs list? Will I ever hold my own children in my arms—or have I completely missed my season to start a family? Will I be cursed with never sharing my life with someone (on the earth) whom I love, cherish, and desire to be with?* I have wondered at times if my desires were ungodly. I have asked myself many of those questions on various days. You may have asked similar questions in your own life.

No, they are not bad desires. They are all godly desires, and that is how God created you to feel, think, and desire. The divine timing of God is always a deep issue for us. I know that God gives us those kinds of desires mentioned above, and I know that those desires honor Him; therefore, they are good in His sight:

> Take delight in the Lord, and He will give you the desires of your heart. (Psalm 37:4 NIV)

Let's pause a moment and pray as we prepare to receive the goodness of the Lord in the land of the living. It's your time! If you can identify with any of the things written in this chapter, you chose the right book. Pause for a moment to say the prayer below:

God of all and the One we honor and adore, you are God. There is no one like you or beside you. You have heard the cries of my heart, and it is my hope that the desires of my heart come to pass. I don't want to always pray for the same thing year after year. Rise up in the midst of my lack and disappointment and show your power. Let your might and power be revealed. Open doors of success and breakthrough, Abba, in my life. Remove the obstacles that are keeping my godly desires away from me. I want a tangible manifestation of them on earth. I believe; therefore, I speak. In the name of Jesus, amen.

Chapter 2

Thriving in the Darkness

Never forget in the dark what God
has promised you in the light.
—Pastor Mike Hayes

Sometimes we experience extreme darkness in our lives. We long to see any good thing come forth. Many times, we feel like we are fighting the water and going against the waves. Through this process, things are transpiring that only God can produce through our extreme circumstances.

When I was in college, during my early twenties, and my mother was on the low end of her long battle with a terminal illness, life came to a screeching halt for me in a few pivotal ways. My grades began to slip tremendously. I found myself growing increasingly dim in my thought process and zest for academic achievement. As a result of seeing myself spiraling downward, I made the difficult decision to drop out of college for a couple of semesters to regroup and gather myself—a do-over if you will.

I was on a "college sabbatical" for about a year before my mother finally went home to be with the Lord. She fought a long fight—a ten-year battle—with various stages of hepatitis and cirrhosis of the liver, which we believe she contracted through a blood transfusion in 1980. On a spring day, the Lord chose a beautiful flower in His garden of humanity to take home and be with Him in heaven—my mother. There were some dark days after this event in my life and the life of my family. My father, the greatest example in my life of a Christian, was shaken to his very core. He was still quite a young man with four children staring at him and looking for answers that no one could satisfy. The next few months and years after my mom's death would prove to be a sink-or-swim time in all our lives.

There were many days of ebb and flow, and I battled denial, depression, weight gain, weight loss, anger, and fear. My desire was simply to have my mom back, but I knew that was not going to happen until we both crossed over into our new heavenly bodies. The anger, resentment, and feelings of abandonment were more than my words can describe. There were times when I felt that life was so jumbled and confusing. I had to make sure I was maintaining a stable state of mind. This proved to be easier said than done at the time. The transition I was experiencing was quite overwhelming. I was working for a small corporation in a college town in Mississippi at that time. I remember sitting at my desk and thinking, *Where is my life going?* There was no chance of upward mobility. I had not graduated from college at that point.

My decision to sit out of college for a couple of semesters when my mother was declining in her health was beginning to impact me. A couple of semesters soon turned into almost three years of academic inactivity. I would frequently hold conversations with vice presidents and other high-ranking people in the small corporation and think, *I am just as smart as they are.* No negative reflection on them, but after each conversation, I knew there was more to my life than talking on a phone with people who seemed ungrateful for my existence. I made the decision to go back to school and finish what I had started.

After I decided to get my education back on track, I contacted my former university to see what I needed to do to resume my studies. I also needed to know how to correct all the errors I had made before leaving the university for my "sabbatical." I was given an advisor to connect with and began my pursuit. The first order of business after I was accepted and registered again was to meet with my advisor and discuss a plan to revisit my "failures" and make them right. Every class I had failed or almost failed had to be retaken. I had to retake several classes to bolster my GPA and get back on track. I spent a year correcting all the mistakes in my classes. As a result, I finally obtained my first college degree.

While working on my degree, I was helping build and develop private elementary schools. Because the school was going through the accreditation process, it was not required that they have a complete staff of licensed teachers. I was selected as a teacher on staff and gained experience in the classroom before getting my degree. I was so grateful for that opportunity, and the pastor who saw the gift in me to afford that opportunity at that time.

I decided not to do my student teaching or practicum, which is the favored way in the education discipline to complete your teaching degree. I was already in the workforce and deeply immersed in bills and responsibilities that many traditional students may not have had. It was a hard decision, but I thought it was the best one at that time. When I informed my advisor that I had decided to pursue the alternative route, which was deciding to override the practicum, he understood, but he was very clearly disappointed. I asked if he thought I was making the wrong decision.

He looked at me and said, "No, this will not stop you from becoming a teacher. I just wanted my son to experience you. You were assigned to his school. My son sometimes struggles in class, and teachers don't always know how to relate to him as a struggling student. I think you would have been a prime source of encouragement for him and could have helped him find his niche in learning. Your patience and understanding would have given him the space to learn in his own way and make him feel like he mattered. I am sad that he will miss that opportunity and encounter with you."

These words from my advisor changed my perspective and outlook in so many ways. Failure leads to success on so many levels, and we don't always see it or understand it completely. I have remembered that over the years, and I have tried my best to work diligently with students to help them discover their own ways of learning. Every person can learn—but not everyone learns the same way.

Chapter 3

The Vision

In their hearts humans plan their course,

but the Lord establishes their steps.

—Proverbs 16:9 (NIV)

One of the things I have learned over the years is that it is important for us to revisit our goals and visions throughout the course of any given year. At the beginning of every year, I write down visions and goals that I would like to see take place and accomplish in that year. I usually start these vision castings around the latter part of December. It's my own personal quirk to have some type of format written out by the end of one year so that I don't come into another year without a road map. I can always make addendums and add things to it as I move into January to make sure I have covered all areas. I sometimes add things throughout the first month. I want to encourage you to do the same in your own life if this is not already a regular practice for you. A road map is very important to have a focused movement throughout the year.

Years ago, I challenged a very outstanding student in my classroom about his plans for college. I challenged him by asking him a few questions. I told him I noticed that he did not have a major according to my roster (it would have been listed on my attendance sheet at the college).

Then I set up a scenario for him to answer a few questions. I asked if he had ever been to California.

He answered, "No, ma'am. I haven't."

I then asked, "If you were going to take a road trip to California, what would be the first thing you would probably want to figure out where you needed to go?"

This was before the days of GPS in cars and on cell phones.

He answered quickly, "I would need a map!"

I responded, "Yes!"

I reminded him since he had never been to California, a road map would be imperative to ensure he arrived at his destination. It would tell him which state highways or interstates to drive. The map would provide clear directions.

I said, "How do you plan to be successful at the university when there is no particular road map for where you're going on *this* journey?"

He smiled and looked at me with his head tilted like the little doggy in the window. "Oh! You are exactly right. I probably need to decide on a major."

Without me saying those exact words, my student understood that he needed direction in order to successfully move through his college tenure. Sometimes, the first year is more about exploration, but a vision should come sooner rather than later to circumvent potholes in that path. I challenged him to make an A in my class, and by the end of the spring semester, I wanted to know what his road map for college would look like. More precisely, I expected him to declare a major!

He smiled, shook my hand, and thanked me for helping him think proactively about his future.

Although it was my expectation, I was pleasantly surprised when that student earned an A in my class. He also informed me on the day of the final that he had updated his college road map. He had declared a major *and* a minor! I smiled brightly and gave him two thumbs-up! I was so proud of him for declaring a vision for his life and for putting a huge stumbling block in the way of the enemy concerning his life. I still challenge my students today. None of us will be able to plan out every step of our lives, but at least we can secure a small road map with vision, goals, and direction for life in that season. God will direct the path in the end.

At the end of the year, it is enlightening and thrilling to see exactly how much has been completed. You may not complete everything on that list, but the things that you do accomplish—from writing the vision and making the vision extremely plain to yourself—are huge! Putting it in the atmosphere and praying over your vision is an act of faith. It is very important to write down those things and make sure they are always before us!

> Then the Lord answered me and said: "Write the vision and make *it* plain on tablets, that he may run who reads it." (Habakkuk 2:2 NKJV)

What is the vision and plan for your life this year? What do you want to accomplish with your family, finances, relationships, career, or education? Have you written it down? Do you speak it over your life daily? Have you committed it to prayer? No one else is going to invest in your life, dreams, and goals more than you can. You must make a framework of what you desire to see and say what you want to see so you can see what you have said (these words come from a song I love).

What exactly does the word vision mean? To clarify one definition of vision act or power of seeing (Merriam-Webster). The Word of God serves as a road map for us and any problems, issues, or situations we encounter. God knows the importance of us having a road map for our lives; therefore, He has left us instructions through His Holy Word.

The Bible is not just for church and learning Bible stories. It is a map to guide us in all things pertaining to life. Vision is very important for obtaining success. If we cannot imagine it in our mind's eyes, more than likely, we will never attain it and see it with our natural eyes. There is power in vision!

Chapter 4

Learning Curve

Everything you need to accomplish

your goals is already in you.

—Anonymous

Life is filled with the hills and valleys of learning opportunities. Some of you are reading this and thinking, *Hills and valleys for sure, but what is the opportunity connected to them?* We must be determined to take the good and bad and make the best of each moment.

No one wakes up and asks for bad things to happen. No one plans bad things, and no one puts bad things on their vision board for the year. However, if you are like me, sometimes in life, Mr. Bad shows up and shows out when he gets there. I have learned so much about how to respond in the recent decades of my life. Prior to these maturing years, my responses usually were not favorable. I spent so much time trying to figure out what, when, and why I had to repeat some things to just pass my test.

As we live in this world, we will experience joy and pain. Happiness and sadness. Disappointments and triumph. None of these moments are greater than God. His ability to comfort, surprise, and answer our prayers with intrinsic detail is still amazing to me.

Regardless of the situation, nothing has exceeded my still, quiet moments with God when He revealed just what I needed.

One of the things I had to learn the hard way was how to enjoy every moment along the way. I really had to receive what God was doing in me. The process He was taking me through was producing the woman He wanted me to be on every level. Like most of us, when the yucky stuff hits the fan, we immediately try to figure out how to get the stink off. How do we make this situation more comfortable and less noticeable?

I didn't realize that God was not concerned about my stinky moments or me being uncomfortable. He wanted to know where my heart was on the situation. If I had done something I shouldn't have—and my ways of error found me—the light now had a place to shine in my space of darkness. Sometimes, it may not have been a consequence of my actions, but a growth spurt does not come without pain. Perhaps you should ask, "What are You doing, God? What are You saying? What am I to learn from this situation?"

My challenge to you is to make sure you pay attention to the learning curve of life. Stop pressing God to change it. Instead, press Him to teach you how to walk through it! Stop wishing it was over—and thank Him for the space of greatness He is propelling you into! Stop whining because Jesus suffered first, and you want to be more like Him, right? Counteract the complaints with speaking life to the hard, despondent places and situations:

> That I may know Him and the power of His resurrection, and the fellowship of His sufferings, being conformed to His death. (Philippians 3:10 NKJV)

He is absolutely a loving God and a perfect parent! He is not sitting on the throne of heaven with a gavel, waiting to sentence you in life. God is filled with more love than your finite mind can conceive of. God is longing to be in relationship with the sons and daughters He created in the Garden of Eden. He is longing to show us how to navigate through the traps of the enemy. He desires to give us success—no matter our mistakes or letdowns in life.

He desires to show us a more excellent way, but we

must be willing to learn. We will *not* have answers about why all the time. Many times, we will not understand the method of what He allows or the timing He allows. However, no one is more powerful or has more authority in heaven and earth than He does. If He allows any movement in my life—whether it be a test from Him or a door that I opened—I am able to conquer it through Christ! He is an amazing God. He created the world with His Word. He has created you with a scoop of dirt from the ground and blew the breath of life into you. Nothing is impossible with God, especially the things that are impossible to humanity:

> In the beginning God created the heavens and the earth. (Genesis 1:1 NKJV)

> In the sweat of your face you shall eat bread till you return to the ground, For out of it you were taken; For dust you are,

And to dust you shall return. (Genesis 3:19 NKJV)

In our lives, we often find ourselves in places we don't like or don't understand. Sometimes we are in a place and cannot fathom how we got there. The decisions we made yesterday are being manifested today. We should always be growing and learning in this journey called life. If you have stopped learning and maturing, it is quite possible that you are dead. If there is nothing else in life to learn, you are probably well on your way out of here.

I want to challenge you to embrace the various seasons of life: the good, the bad, the ugly, and the indifferent. Challenge your perception of what you see and think during these times. I do not speak this callously or without my own experiences that I wanted to take back to Walmart and get a refund or a gift card. My pastor said that our attitudes determine our altitudes. It hit me like a boulder at that point in my life. I am sure I knew it on some level in my mind, but having it said that way was so perfect and timely.

When I hit an unwanted space and could not figure out what had happened to get me there, I actively engaged God with serious prayer and dialogue. I actively inquired about what He wanted me to learn. Perception is everything. When I paced myself a little differently than in the past, I noticed my anxiety levels beginning to balance out. It did not make the trials any easier. I still sat and cried, leaned heavily on Jesus, and thanked Him when I didn't know what else to do, but His faithfulness showed up every time.

My challenge to you is to step up on the inside. We seem to have perfected doing things so that others can see and know what we are doing well. That, within itself, comes with an immediate reward. Stand when your knees are weak, pursue vision when your eyes are cloudy, and love and trust when your heart is faint. Stand up with strategic intention to please God in all things. Check your heart during prayer. Check your motives before you get dressed. Check your attitude at the door. God is very intentional with what He is doing in all things. This is how we learn to navigate the learning curves of our lives:

> But as for you, you meant evil against me; but God meant it for good, in order to bring it about as it is this day, to save many people alive. (Genesis 50:20 NKJV)

There is nothing happening or going on in your life that God is not aware of. Sometimes, we think that God will skip the consequences of our poor decisions because He is forgiving, but this is not true. He is certainly able to endow us with mercy, but consequences will arise after any decision—good, bad, or ugly.

When I was in college, we used to say, "Check yourself before you wreck yourself." I am sure that puts me right in the late eighties and early nineties! It is so true—even more than we know. We thought it was a cute little trendy saying, but the truth of the matter is that we need to always check ourselves to make sure we are operating with wisdom and godly intentions.

> For the Lord searches all hearts and understands all the intent of the thoughts. If you seek Him, He will be found by you; but if you forsake Him, He will cast you off forever. (1 Chronicles 28:9b NKJV)

Once our hearts, motives, and intentions are in the right place, we don't have to worry about pleasing other people. We will move by God's instructions and His might. We will engage better and more thoroughly in His will and His desires for our lives. We will make fewer mistakes because of our pure motives. We will always make mistakes, but we will mature in them and recuperate better from them when our hearts are aligned with the Word of God.

I often hear people say that people cannot change, but I disagree. I have changed in many ways over the years, and I know many other people who have changed. However, the change started on the inside, and then it progressed to the outside. I think the problem with people trying to change is how they pursue it and the motives behind it. It must start inwardly, and then it will spread wherever it is needed.

Intention plays a strong role in this process too. Intent should be accompanied by practice, and what we practice will manifest itself through active behaviors. If your intent is to change and the practice of that behavior is engaged, then change will come.

Chapter 5

Derailing Disappointment

Life is all about setbacks. A life lived without disappointment is a life lived in a cocoon. People have recovered from far worse setbacks.

—Tony Clark

Just stop and take a deep breath after reading the title and quote introducing this chapter. There is that heavy, weighty, and scary word we are all too familiar with: "disappointment." I read a definition of this word that really sums it up: "the act or an instance of disappointing; the state or emotion of being disappoints" (Merriam-Webster).

Does that sound familiar to any of you out there?

Life is sure to bring us a few things with certainty. You will pay taxes, you will eventually die off this earth, and you will experience disappointment in your lifetime! There is nothing like the daunting feeling it brings and how it lingers when it shows up. It is like stumbling upon a cactus plant. I have never encountered one that didn't leave a sting!

I have been disappointed by friends, loved ones, coworkers, co-laborers in ministry, myself, and even God (because He didn't do it my way). No matter how many times disappointment shows up, the pain that it releases is still the same! You yelp, kick, and scream. You ask yourself why and how. You analyze and revisit, trying to see which wrong turn you made on the road of life. You cry and give up, and then you start again to see if you can remove yourself from its relentless grip.

Our level of disappointment begins with our level of expectation. I have witnessed so many situations and circumstances over the years, and I know that there are so many unanswered questions in the minds of people everywhere about their disappointments.

I experienced a devastating tragedy while in college, and I want to give you a little background so that you will have more insight about what I was going through as I maneuvered through that time of grief. My mother passed away during my undergraduate years at college. She was young and vibrant, and she had a godly husband and four children. She also had a great relationship with the Lord. When I was in sixth grade, my mother had an episode of sickness that the doctors could not explain at first. At the time, none of the doctors could really articulate what may have been the issue. We eventually found out that she had contracted a serious viral disease, hepatitis, which would eventually cause cirrhosis of the liver and end her life.

A couple of years prior to that diagnosis, my mother had given birth to my baby sister, and we almost lost her in that birthing process. She required large blood transfusions to maintain life. She contracted hepatitis, which we resolved was a result of the blood transfusions. Her lifestyle did not reflect the disease, and my father did not have the disease. This was prior to the outbreak of deadlier diseases, and all the protocols for donated blood drastically changed after we became more knowledgeable about them. A hidden disease was possibly lurking in one of those transfusions.

Her body went through so many changes. The Bible teaches us that "life" is in the blood, yet I watched her very life source of blood slowly but surely causing her death. She was in a coma in the hospital for about seven days. The doctors were at a loss about what to do and how to treat her. They didn't know what the problem was and or what to do with her.

I remember my father's prayers. He was and still is a praying man, and he prayed so diligently for my mom when the doctors couldn't do anything because they had no idea about her condition. My mother was a very quiet spirit, a great mom, and a wonderful wife. She was loved by everyone who knew her. She had the sweetest disposition. She was docile and lovable in all her ways. For those who know me personally, I am just like my father! That is my story, and I am sticking with it.

She battled the disease for eleven years. There were many trips to the emergency room and many hospital stays and visits before we got to the end of her journey. I vividly remember her last week of life. We mapped out a plan of who would stay with her and comfort her during what would unfortunately turn out to be her last round in the hospital. Her sister Mary took the first week, and I took the second week. My mom's niece would be taking a third week if necessary. We had our schedules, and we were set and ready for the ebb and flow of how things normally took place. My father worked and would come on the weekends to stay with her and visit throughout the week.

I made full use of the chapel in the hospital. During that time, I discovered the gift of intercession. I carried it inside, and it slowly rose to the top. I cried out in deep supplication to the Lord on behalf of my mother every day. She sat quietly in her bed, watching her surroundings, and gazed at me and the doctors and nurses. I often wondered what thoughts were going through her head during that phase of her sickness.

She didn't talk much or engage consistently. Every day, I would walk from her room down to the chapel and fall on my knees at the altar before God and ask him to heal my mother, to save her life, to renew her strength, and to restore her body. Every day that week, I prayed and asked God to do this for our family. When I came back up from my prayers, I watched her for the remainder of the day. Her condition and behavior remained the same. I was amazed at her endurance and stamina. There was so much prodding and poking by the doctors and nurses. Anyone who has ever spent any time in the hospital knows there is no rest for the weary there. There are times when I would see her facial expression reflecting the pain in her body, but she never opened her mouth and never complained. She kept a consistent smile on her face with all visitors and family. She was a fighter if I have ever seen one. She was a warrior to the end!

That weekend, as my Dad came in, I prepared to go back to my college town for work. It turned into the worst weekend of my life. I woke up on Saturday morning and got dressed for work. I was feeling extremely heavy in my spirit. It felt like something was hanging on my back. I was so sad, but I could not explain why I was crying. I called my dad and asked him to let me speak with my mom. He paused for a moment, and there was silence on the other end of the phone. My heart skipped a beat.

He finally said, "Well, I think you should get back over to the hospital as soon as you can."

My insides felt weak. I was in another state and was about an hour and a half away. My dad told me that my mom had been quiet all day. She had absolutely refused to talk to anyone on the phone—even her own mother—and he felt like she was slipping away from him. He asked me to get there as quickly as I could if I could find a way. At the time, I did not have a car. I would have to depend on someone to take me back to Mobile, Alabama, in order to get there promptly. What a gloomy day that was in every way. I couldn't stop crying, and I didn't have the transportation to get where I needed to go! I was the definition of *helpless* in that moment! I remember it like it was yesterday, and the hurt is just as real.

That evening, after working my shift, some friends from church offered to drive me to Mobile. The drive from Hattiesburg to Mobile that day was the longest drive of my life.

I felt the heaviness hitting me with each mile marker on highway 98. My heart began to grow heavier as we got closer to the hospital. We finally reached Mobile, and as we were coming to a traffic light in front of the hospital, the tears rolled down my cheeks. In that moment, I knew my mother was gone from this world.

As we were sitting at the traffic light, I lifted my head and looked at my three friends. I said, "She didn't make it. I didn't even get a chance to say goodbye."

They all said, "No—don't say that! We believe. We believe! She is still going to be alive when you get there, and you'll get a chance to say your goodbyes."

I knew in my *knower*—another word for gut feeling in Mississippi—that she had gone to be with Jesus. I told them to drop me off in front of the hospital, and one of them jumped out with me to go up to her room. It was on the fifth floor. I can remember it so clearly. On the elevator, you could have heard a pin drop on carpet. When the elevator reached the fifth floor, I rushed toward her hospital room. I could hear someone calling my name from the opposite end of the hallway. My dad was calling out to me and asking me to wait.

I stopped and slowly turned around.

He walked up to me, grabbed my shoulders, and looked straight into my eyes. "She's gone. Your mama is gone. She didn't get to see you make it back."

At that moment, my life changed forever!

How in the world would I go on in life? How could I live and be successful without my mother? Who would help me and guide me when I lost my way? Who would comfort me when I was confused and not sure of what to do? Who would assure me that love would come again and that he would be the right one for me? Who would assure me that I would make a great wife and mother? Who would affirm me and tell me I am doing a great job in my career—even when I question things going on? Who would do this for me like only a mother could?

This event derailed the hope in the foundation of my family's faith. My father's strength and resilience experienced a massive shift. My brother's hope and purpose encountered many battles and bruises for years. Would he ever reclaim the person he was created to be—or would he remain in a state of unrest and defiance? My sisters experienced a deep space of deprivation because they got the least amount of time with her. Would they ever know how much she loved them? Would they ever know their purpose in life? How would this deep hole in their lives be filled?

The family of Deacon A. L. Packer needed God in those times; otherwise, we would not survive. It was time to put our faith to work and really lean in on the Word of God and His peace and presence. I had prayed so hard for God to spare my mother's life and keep her around to see all her children flourish, including me. I had prayed for her to see me get married and have my own kids.

I had prayed for divine healing in her body and for the restoration and renewal of all organs. He was God, and if anyone could renew and restore, it would be Him and Him alone. I had basically asked God for a miracle concerning her life, and what I got was her death! The next few days, months, and years would be quite a journey. So, we forged ahead the best way we knew how—one rocky day at a time.

There were many days when I screamed, yelled, and became discontented with my life and the things in it. I threw myself into a frenzy of work and ministry, but none of that filled the void of my mother's death. I had my good days and not-so-good days in my relationship with the Lord. After all, I felt like it was His fault (as the grieving stages would direct me to believe). He could have stopped it at any time, and I would still have a mother. She would still be alive! Those were my grieving thoughts and feelings at that time. I am sure I hit every level of the grieving stages that first year!

My family experienced many cracks in our foundation during that first year or so, but we managed to hang on to God despite the result that we absolutely did not care for. My mother and father did a wonderful job in giving us a godly foundation. I am grateful for that every day of my life. We all felt like we were experiencing a few days of Job's life (if we can dare to compare our single loss to his loss of everything). The loss was so deep. The grieving process is such a huge giant to contend with.

There were many peaks and valleys as we worked our way back to a family after having our center torn apart from us. We experienced a minor falling away from my dad when he simply stepped away from church for a small season. My brother went off the rails in his own way and tried every form of comfort besides Jesus. My sisters engaged in their own form of comfort, which we could have never guessed or seen coming before my mom's death. I, as the firstborn, was the surrogate mother—not by choice! I was trying to hold it all together, and I never properly grieved. It was a major dysfunction. It was the perfect space for God to step into our lives, and we needed Him to do so quickly.

Everyone will take their own path to grieve and handle it to the best of their ability. If God is not deleted from your process, you will come back to center more easily and quickly. Our roots were so deep in God that no matter which wrong turn we took, we all ended up back at our center and in the face of God!

I know my brother tried his best to vacate his godly roots, but if you talk to him today, you will get a mini sermon and lots of encouragement. You will know you have been in the presence of a man who loves God and follows after Him greatly! One of my sisters who derailed in high school and had us frantically looking for her all night long one weekend is now a godly mother of four. Her wonderful husband is a leader in their church. My other sister started her family without a husband, and she is a poster child for what a single mother is capable of. She completed her bachelor's degree and master's degree while raising little kids alone. She has a great job that she loves as a counselor, and she has raised warriors for the kingdom! She is a great mother and an awesome woman of God. She teaches and preaches the Gospel. My dad was back "deaconing" in the church within two years after my mom's transition! He is the same stately example I have always remembered having, and he is making an even greater impact at seventy years old! I am amazed by his stamina and his flourishing gift from God!

And then there is me. It is my desire to please God in all things, but I feel and know I fail more than I care to admit. I pray that I am learning with each rise and fall. The opportunity to speak to women and empower them is always near me, and I thank God each and every time I have the opportunity to do so. Each day of my life has purpose and destiny—whether I feel it or not. That belief always keeps me centered, focused, and rising to the occasion. I finally reached a place to grieve safely and express my thoughts and feelings and not feel judged for them. I am grateful for my journey. I am thankful for divine connections and authentic, supportive relationships along the way. I am in one of the healthiest places of my life—physically, mentally, and spiritually—as a result of my acute attention to pending issues on the inside. Be true to yourself! Healing starts on the inside.

Chapter 6

Capturing the Moment

Happy moments, *praise* God. Difficult moments, *seek* God. Quiet moments, *worship* God. Painful moments, *trust* God. Every moment, *thank* God.

—Rick Warren

You may be currently living in the chapter of disappointment, but don't miss what God is doing now! My challenge to you is to find the place where God is working and capture that moment right now. I learned how to do this the hard way. Sometimes, I am distracted by the chaos of what may seem like confusion, and I miss the moment. God has been so faithful to keep me in the presence of great people who remind me to capture the moment of where I am while they also speak wellness to my long-awaited dreams and desires.

I am still single at the time of writing this book, yet my desire to be married, which has not wavered since I was twenty-three, is still there. I honestly do not share that in conversation with most people. My inner circle and the people who actually listen to me in conversations about my desires and goals in life are the ones who hear the most about it. I have learned that many people will respond according to their own despondency and disappointments, and they will inadvertently speak negatively about your desires. If you are reading this book, I don't mind sharing it with you because you likely have your own dreams. I will wait with you, and I support your dreams and desires. I will speak life to your dreams, and I will pray that you speak life to mine. If more people would respond like that to the sharing of our heart, that would bring healing and a level of comfort while we wait.

I have begun to develop steady and deeper relationships in Texas. I am from a small town in Mississippi, but I moved to Texas in 2007. I have been in Texas for thirteen years, and I really can't believe it has been that long. There have been so many winding roads, but I have also encountered vast spaces of revelation, growth, and maturity. I can honestly say I am thankful for it all.

I am thankful for it all, but that does not mean I want to repeat any of the winding roads, heartaches, mishaps, or jacked-up places in my life from the past decade. I have developed the mind-set of learning the lesson as I walked through those dark times. I hope I will not be repeating those same mistakes. Not everything was a mistake of choice, but God allowed me to travel through those places to learn the lessons He wanted to teach me.

This southern girl with a big personality really had a hard time developing friendships when I moved to Texas. I didn't have a problem meeting people or getting along with people, which is part of my natural personality. I can talk to a mannequin, and it just might respond! I am a people person. I have never had a problem connecting with introverts or extroverts, but I found myself not allowing people into my friendship zone. I kept them at arm's length for sure. As a result, I encountered various bouts of loneliness and even some depression. I would work hard to escape the depression and oppression because it always led to nowhere, and I was smart enough to realize that. I hate being depressed, and I am a fighter without reservation when it shows up! I keep my prayer books and journals ready for activation in any challenging space. They are some of my tools of choice! There is nothing like a good prayer in tongues to confuse the demon of depression!

Once I finally got past my space of resistance and shutting out new friends, I totally embraced my new home in Texas. I was thankful to experience the team on my first "real" job in Texas at a middle school at a Christian Academy. The whole atmosphere at that school was about winning for us all. No one was better than anyone else, and when one teacher won, we all won! If one was down, we all worked to pull him or her back up. It was a defining moment in my life because I'd had a few conversations with God about possibly never working in Christian environments again due to the disappointment and confusion I had experienced before I left Mississippi. He totally redeemed all of that, and I am so thankful for that!

During the past few years, I have really worked on intentionally developing friendships. It's become a mantra. I like to connect with people who are going somewhere. Always wishing, hoping, and talking is not the way to expand faith or reach goals. I am attracted to people who inspire me to move forward, take a chance, and not fear failure. I am thankful for every person who has encouraged me in my most despondent moments—and there have been many— to keep going.

So many times, we seem to be waiting for the right moment. Perhaps when we get more money or when things get to a better place in our lives, we will help or become involved. I say start where you are. If you are like the rest of us, life runs in ebbs and flows. When I don't have the extra money to give, I usually have time to give. When I don't have extra time, I may have extra money, and I give that. Perhaps I can cook a meal if I don't have either of those. There are so many ways we can give of ourselves and capture the moment in our lives. I encourage you to actively seek a way to give more of you. There is a way you can contribute. There is no better time than the present.

Today, I am still capturing the moment. It is a

Sunday evening, and I am looking out on the gorgeous view of where I live. I attended service this morning and decided to take a slow walk out of church. I stopped and spoke to several people on my way out. I had meaningful conversations, and it felt good to not rush. I loathe rushing. It is the quickest way to death in my opinion. I am so glad to be out of the rushing phase of my life. I am shaking my head just thinking about it. What was I thinking during that decade of my life? I was probably trying to impress somebody. For whatever reason, we are always rushing for others—not really ourselves. I don't miss it at all!

My dreams and desires are still the same, but I will not wallow in self-pity. I want to make the most of every moment on this journey. You may get tired of the wait and wonder why, but don't stop living. Keep your face north. Keep your prayers going. Stand—without wavering—on God's Word! Enjoy every day until you get there because we cannot come back to this moment.

Make memories and share life with those who want to share life with you. If someone is pushing you out of their life, it is their loss. It can be hard for us to accept that. Knock the dust off your feet and keep moving. You have a choice of connecting where you want to connect, and they do too. If you are getting pushback, bless them and move on. Don't make a spectacle of them—or of you. Don't develop a bad attitude or talk about them to your circle of friends.

Sometimes, people are not ready for what you have to offer. I have encountered people who were not ready for real, authentic, godly love. They were more comfortable with love that was conditional and based on what they could do for the other person. They were more comfortable with someone loving them because of their money, status, or position because they knew what to expect. Since I chose to love genuinely and simply, it was hard for them to receive me. They preferred deception and lies to authenticity.

I have a tendency to love people where they are. This does not always make it easier, and I sometimes struggle with loving people because it is an effort. I understand that they can only love as great or as genuine as their relationship with God. The world will give us a certain measure for love, but my measure is based on the Word of God. I lean in heavily on Him to help me do this. It is impossible without His help!

One of my favorite authors enlightened me about how God loves us. I strongly believe and know from my life that God loves us all uniquely. We all have different needs, and God is great at meeting us wherever we are.

Chapter 7

Unconditional

The measure of love is to love without measure.

—St. Francis de Sales

Many times in our lives, we are paralyzed by failure. This the response that the enemy of our destiny likes to see in us. The adversary (the devil) desires that we get stuck, remain immobile, and are hinged in fear so that we can never reach our fullest potential in life. He desires to poke fun at us, laugh in our ears, and cause us to stay in a perpetual state of self-doubt. This is the main focus that he desires, but it is not the plan that God has for our lives.

Everything about God is about multiplication and

progress. If we are not progressing, we are immobile. If we are not multiplying something in our lives— finances, coaching, mentoring, or growing internally— we are stagnant. If we are not still dreaming and pursuing those dreams, we are more than likely paralyzed in fear. God always has more, better, and greater for us. We never have to wonder or fear that He isn't concerned for us. He is, without doubt, longing to give us good gifts. God loves us so much that He will sometimes handpick a perfect setup for us to see if we will respond to His love.

I dated someone in college, and many years later, we encountered each other again. He had experienced some dark times in his life during that in-between space. I, too, had experienced many pitfalls and much darkness, but I was very stable in my relationship with the Lord. I was in a thriving space spiritually when we reconnected. He was learning to trust God again and was struggling with that trust. I could tell that by how he responded to my love, care, and concern. We really do treat others the way we treat God in many ways. He was very resistant, mostly out of fear of being too vulnerable, and he struggled with receiving a godlike kind of love. He was so used to conditional love based on works or what he could do for others, and it simply broke my heart to see and hear his struggle with it. I never required him to do anything special for my love. He was very loving to me and gracious in many ways. Whether he received it or not, my love was consistent. God loves us the same way! Many people suffer from not knowing a godly kind of love. The Almighty God. Jehovah Shalom. Prince of Peace. Wonderful Counselor. Elohim.

God's love for us remains even in our good, bad, dark, and sad times. When we are thick in sin and making horrible decisions, God is there. When we are doubting Him and His love for us because we are still praying the same prayers that haven't been answered twenty years later, God is there. When we are filled with judgment and self-righteousness, God is there. When we are unsure, uncertain, and don't know, God is there. When we lose loved ones, and they were "good people," "so young," "my only child," or by a "senseless tragedy," God is still there.

In the midst of the deepest tragedies, our truest selves come forth. You must allow God to perfect you and mold you in those times. It is not easy. He is usually the one we are most angry with, and our natural tendency is to pull away from Him. However, my challenge to you would be to migrate to Him to see if He is who He proclaims to be and if He can do what he says He can do.

The God we serve and tell everyone about is who we are expecting to show up on our behalf. He alone can make the impossible possible. Just like Moses reminding God that his reputation was on the line if he killed the Israelites and started over, I begin to remind God of His promises. There are witnesses to some promises. Your reputation is on the line. My hope and trust are in You. You promised to give me the desires of my heart if I served you and humbled myself before you. I have done what you have asked as best as I could, and I know that you are not cruel. I am imperfect, and You are perfect in all Your ways. You have said I would be surprised, yet I only feel disappointment. God, only You can make my dreams come true and cause all the divine movements to come to order and move me into a place of coronation.

Learning to pray God's Word back to Him is extremely important because He honors His Word. Following His commandment of loving our neighbors as we love ourselves takes much effort. We must love others as we love ourselves, which is something to contemplate. The guy I dated could not adequately receive my love and care for himself. It reflected his inability to love and receive from God and the way he felt about himself. The deep place of self-hatred, condemnation, and guilt that had built up over the years caused a wall in the relationship that no one could breach but God. It literally appeared in many of his relationships from my observation.

> And the second, like *it, is* this: "You shall love your neighbor as yourself." There is no other commandment greater than these." (Mark 12:31 NKJV)

There is a clear difference in selfishness and self-love. Self-love is highly motivated from a healthy space, and our decisions are usually influenced by the presence of loved ones and our love for them. Selfishness is complete tunnel vision. No other factors are considered, and the damage along the way is not considered until the consequences arrive.

Chapter 8

I Like You!

A man cannot be comfortable

without his own approval.

—Mark Twain

I contemplated not putting this chapter in my book because I wasn't sure if it could possibly help anyone or if it was simply my personal issue and victory. Many of us, especially women, go through times of discovery in our twenties. There is something about those years of trying to become an adult that really highlights the need to figure out this thing called life. We are navigating the early roads of life and discovering who we are. For me, it probably started in high school.

I have always been a face value type of person. My personality is such that I honestly treat people the way I want to be treated.

I am not good at mind games, tricks, or manipulation. I didn't grow up in a household that promoted that, and I never learned an all-around prosperous use for it. I do my best to stay on level ground. That does not mean that people did not use these measures against me at times. I have fallen victim more often than I care to admit. Most people would say I was naive. That is possibly truer than I would have cared to admit during my high school and college years. However, I do understand that what we sow, we will reap! I will leave that right there.

I remember a few encounters in high school, college, and early adulthood where two green-eyed monsters—envy and jealousy—would appear to challenge me more often than I cared to deal with. The demonic force that made its way to the forefront depended on the situation.

Most ladies will be able to relate to someone being jealous of their hair, clothes, or popularity. I am not sure if my hair was anything to rave about, although I did get quite a few compliments since I loved wearing it big in the eighties. I still love big hair! My clothes were nothing to brag about because I was very inept at the latest styles, and we lived very modestly. I wore quite a few hand-me-downs, and popularity was what the people wanted at that moment in time. The good old days of hormonal high school were filled with its ebb and flow.

My greatest recollection of these green-eyed monsters wasn't clear until college and a few years after college. Once I was able to look back on some things, it totally made sense. My encounter with the green-eyed beast was really about the things I could not order out of a catalog (online shopping wasn't as popular yet), pick up from Walmart, or go into a beauty spa and walk out with a new and improved one. The things that seemed to really cause people to shun or reject me were my personality, character, integrity, kindness, and genuine attitude. I received so much blatant rejection and unkind treatment because many people had issues with the person I was and still am. It was quite confusing. Being as naive as I was, I had a terrible time understanding why people responded to me in such a different, almost offensive way.

I also came across people who had a problem with the physical me. I was never a single-digit size. I have been a double-digit girl since middle school, but my family has always very supportive of who I am. I was not an unhealthy weight at the time, and in my home, there were no issues with my double digits. The issues would transpire outside of my home. I remember comments and snide remarks. I remember people making "suggestions" about my need to "shave off a few." I remember it being attached to the reason I "may not be able to get a husband." It has been attached to why I "may not be able to have children." You name it, my weight has been a way to demean, degrade, and denigrate me.

I want to encourage all the ladies reading this who may be slightly fluffier than the single-digit girl at work. You are wonderfully made and fierce in all your ways. There will never be another you. If you want to make changes in those double digits, the power to do so may be in your control. If not, own it and move forward. I never dated or encountered anyone who was interested in me for a date or relationship who had a problem with my weight. There was never a mean word or an inference of me "needing" to lose weight. I am very thankful for that because I realize some men are verbally abusive in that way. If you are in a relationship where that is going on, walk away. If you are dating, you deserve better. If you are married to him, please work on communication regarding this. Perhaps a conversation is all it takes. If it is really out of bounds, pray and fast for God to deal with his heart! Only God can change a heart. You can talk until you're blue in the face, but until the heart is right, the words will produce a hard landing and mostly be received offensively.

I am so thankful for parents who gave me stability and taught me how to confidently be who I am. I had to really wrap my head around why mean girls and even adults would have issues with me for what seemed to be no reason. They didn't understand my kindness, respect for others, or lack of need to be someone other than myself.

By the end of my twenties, I had had enough of the cacophony! I was quite focused on my plans for the next five to seven years of my life, and I wanted to move into my destiny and reach my goals. I remember the day when a great revelation hit me. My little apartment was tucked away on a little street in the college town where I lived. I woke up one morning, looked into the mirror, pointed to myself, and said, "I like you!"

When I was twenty-eight, I was introduced to a tall, dark, and handsome man who was coming to visit me for the first time. I wore jeans, a cute little blouse, and some cute little flats. Flats are my absolute favorite comfort-wear shoes, especially since I am five foot ten and three-quarters. As I finished with a smidgen of makeup and a smear of lip gloss, I knew life would not be the same from that day forward. I have not looked back or given any more thought to the opinions of others. They no longer take up space in my thoughts.

In a conversation with my date that evening, he mentioned how easy it was for him to be in my company. He said that I showed so much confidence in who I was. He also said most women would be so keen on trying to impress that it would cause much awkwardness, but he was impressed that I was comfortable being me. As a result, he said it made him comfortable with being him. I simply thanked God inwardly. Little did he know how that morning I had jumped a huge hurdle to reclaim my confidence. Our relationship did not go any further than dating. I am not sure I know why, but the things that people are most attracted to about you can also be a source of contention. Perhaps that was his take on us. He was kind and good to me.

For as he thinks in his heart, so is he. (Proverbs 23:7 NKJV)

I will praise You, for I am fearfully and wonderfully made; Marvelous are Your works, And that my soul knows very well. (Psalm 139:14 NKJV)

Be the person God created you to be, and always be evolving into a better version of you. I really hope you allow that to resonate in your spirit. We live in a world where few people are satisfied with who they are, and many people spend a lifetime trying to be someone else or satisfy people they don't even care to be around. This is not living a full and abundant life. In fact, it sounds quite miserable to never fully live your life and be who you were created to be.

God didn't make a mistake, and you were not born into the wrong family. You were born with a purpose in mind. Our Creator can transform our mistakes, bloopers, blunders, catastrophic errors, and major failures and turn them into something beautiful. He is the same God who watched over Moses as he was released into the river by his mother to save his life and eventually ended up being raised in the house of Pharaoh.

He is the same God who positioned Joseph to be raised up as the governor of Egypt after his brothers sold him to foreigners and lied to their father by reporting that he had been killed by a wild animal. Joseph would eventually save their lives in the midst of a famine because He was in charge of the food supply during the drought!

He is the same God who protected Sarah when her husband, Abraham, lied about his relationship with her. The king desired to have her as his own, but God intervened through a tumultuous dream and caused the king to release her back to her husband before any harm or shame was done.

He is the same God who saved the life of Rahab, a harlot, who did not worship Him but highly feared Him and opened her house as a place of safety for the Israelite spies as they were chasing the promised land.

He is the same God who gave Queen Esther favor in the sight of the king and saved the lives of a generation of Jews as Haman devised a plan to kill them all under the reign of this king.

He is the same God who redeemed and blessed Jacob after he swindled his own brother and stole his birthright. He is the same God who lovingly forgave

Peter after he denied Him three times in the courtyard when Jesus was being tried and headed for crucifixion.

Yes, the God we serve knows you better than you know yourself. He knows your capability of making mistakes—even though it is His desire that we make the wise choice. He is a God of free will and will allow you to make the choice of your heart. Right or wrong, He is standing right there to walk you through. It may be hard and arduous, but He will be with you. He will not leave you. You have been so delicately fashioned that no one else has your fingerprint, and no one else has your eye pattern. Your retina scan is unique to you. Your fingerprint is your own. Your footprint is your own as well. These are delicate details that only a great and mighty God could accomplish for all the billions of people on the planet!

I don't want you to find yourself in a place where you are settling for less than you deserve. I am a firm believer that if my motives line up with the Word of

God, it is certainly a desire that God has given me. If God has given me the desire, I know that He gives great gifts. They are full and complete, and they add no sorrow. Reach out for the fullness of what God has promised you. Stand on His Word and draw from it daily. He never lies or has to repent for what He has said.

You can have the desires of your heart. It is His pleasure to give His children gifts—just like it is your pleasure to give gifts to your children, friends, and loved ones.

I often run into women my age or a little younger who deeply desire husbands and families. Unfortunately, they are not always comfortable with admitting their desires in the Christian world because fellow believers are so intent on "fixing" them or the perceived issue. I totally understand because I have experienced the same thing from Christians. I have learned not to engage with some of them because you will have to get saved all over again at the end of that conversation. I quickly move on so that I am not overanalyzed or given a diagnosis. In the meantime, we keep living, working, worshipping, and doing the work of the ministry at whatever level we serve. We pray and believe God will cause the encounter, and that could be anywhere or at any time. I know godly men shop, eat, go to the park, and walk on the sidewalk. Therefore, I never limit God on where one of His sons may show up. My prayer is for God to orchestrate the meeting. We will both draw on Him for the rest.

I once attended a wedding that was such a blessing to witness. My friend married the love of her life on a beautiful fall evening. The wedding had been long anticipated. I am sure she felt like it would never come to fruition due to the turbulence they experienced for a few unfortunate reasons. It was as if one day, the Lord allowed her current husband's heart to open and receive her as the gift she was and is. Nothing could stop him from moving forward and making her his wife. He didn't look to the left or to the right. He focused on choosing and loving his wife-to-be.

At the reception, her sister made a toast and said something I will never forget. It has resonated with me in my prayers for my future husband. Her sister complimented the couple, welcomed her new brother into the family, and thanked him for loving her sister so well.

Wow! That was my response in my spirit and in my words! Everything in my spirit leaped and jumped for joy because that was a defining word and moment. I thought, *Lord, yes. I thank you that my husband will love me well.*

I am not perfect, but when I am loved well. I will be perfect for him. I am not without mistakes, but I can apologize and learn to do it better when I am loved well. We all can in any relationship! I cannot promise to be excellent in all things, but I will become a better version of me for the sake of our relationship when I am loved well.

Basically, we all require something different in how we like to be loved. I want to encourage you to know that God desires to connect us with mates who love us well. This doesn't mean that you don't need to improve or grow—always work on growth and maturity—but know that God desires for your mate to love you well as you love him well too! Never have an expectation that you don't plan to meet yourself. Things change quickly in life, and some situations can cause us to stand in a space that we didn't plan for, but with God, all things are possible. With God, we can all love each other well.

Loving your mate well always begins with loving yourself well. Knowing who you are in Christ and knowing how much He loves you will bring a great amount of peace and resolve to loving yourself. Loving God, keeping a healthy, connected relationship with Him, and loving yourself are great building blocks for any relationship. God created you in His image.

Chapter 9

Savvy Success

You are braver than you believe, stronger than
you seem, and smarter than you think.

—Winnie the Pooh

Savvy is a word that I really liked the sound of when
I first heard it. I wasn't exactly sure what it meant,
but I had always been pretty keen on figuring it out
by context or how it was used. To help you skip that
part, I will tell you the meaning of it. Savvy means
having or showing perception, comprehension, or
shrewdness in practical matters (Merriam-Webster).
I am definitely more astute in some areas than others.

Being equipped with this skill has been a blessing to me and others over the years.

One of the things I want to challenge you on in this chapter is your savviness. I am a firm believer that we should all be lifelong learners no matter how much we have struggled in the past. I struggled for many years of my adult life and into recent years with trying to make sense of some of my financial aspects. I always felt inept. It was not because I was not frugal or spent carelessly, but I really didn't have an understanding how money worked for me.

For as long as you live on this earth, you will need money to meet basic life needs such as shelter, food, gas, and medicine. No matter how much you love Jesus, the doctor is still expecting a payment for his service, and if there is a hospital visit, they will bill you if there is no insurance—or you will be billed for anything the insurance doesn't pay. The bank or mortgage company may have a few Christian employees, but if your mortgage is not kept current, it will eventually go into foreclosure. You may try waltzing into your local supermarket singing psalms and hymns and thinking they will give you groceries, but your basket will go from full to empty as you waltz back to your car after leaving the basket of unpaid groceries at the register. Of course, there is always room for miracles and favors, but daily living does require a measure of money.

I have been on a journey to figure out how this money thing works for me since I moved Texas. I was so excited that I was part of a church that offered so many classes to help us in various areas of our lives, and we could take as many as we could stand any given year. Once I settled in, I immediately joined a financial class that was very valuable and taught me quite a bit about how to pay attention to my finances. It brought about a keen awareness of how I was spending my money and potential ways to save my money.

I learned how to review my bank statement since it is always ready and available online—even if your last transaction was fifteen minutes ago. Discovering my spending habits was a very sobering experience. I knew some things were going to have to change. The class also laid out a plan to pay off debt and become free of debt. Retirement and investments were also discussed. However, my immediate plan was to make my money work for me on a daily basis. I learned quite a bit from that first class, but the next class taught me how to live financially well.

I didn't sign up for the next class experience, but I was at my wit's end while making a huge transition into part of my dream job. Due to huge financial changes accompanying that move, I was in a very low and despondent place. I had a conversation with a friend and explained how I felt.

She looked at me, tilted her head to the side, and said, "Hold on one minute."

I felt like the emoji where the girl is sitting with both palms held up and her shoulders shrugged.

I had no idea what she was talking about as she went upstairs to her office. When she came back to the cafe where we had been chatting, she had a huge smile on her face and was carrying a big rectangular box. I saw a very familiar face on the box. I smiled and took the box that would begin a journey of financial peace. She told me it was a gift and explained that she had been trying to figure out who to give it to. I guess the timing of my complaint was perfect. Imagine that!

I cannot accurately articulate how amazing this personal study would be for me. I was in such a place of desperation that I engulfed everything quite quickly over the next month. I read the book in a weekend. I did not complete the workbook because I thought it was part of a DVD class session. I scrounged through the box, found a small binder of CDs, and hit another level of absorption.

I had a thirty-minute commute to work each day, and I listened to each CD twice to make sure I didn't miss anything. Not all the lessons were for me, but I actively applied all that I could. I put my plan into motion!

By no means have I arrived at how to perfectly handle money, but my relationship with it has changed. I am no longer estranged from it. I learned several practical steps to steadily meet my goals. I began to experience new levels of financial freedom. My anxiety levels dropped tremendously, and I allowed the Holy Spirit to empower me more with the teachings I had receiving from this personal study.

About a year later, I needed an updated car. My old one was about ten years old and had almost two hundred thousand miles. It had maxed out on its mileage and ability to keep me safe while commuting. As I pursued this update, I learned to maintain boundaries on my budget and the art of how to negotiate, negotiate, and negotiate. And that I did. After receiving the dollar amount from the Lord, I set my budget for the small transaction, and I do mean small. My budget was secured and met! God did more than I could even conceive of with my budget. I am still in awe of His movement in that transaction.

I believe that it is God's will to walk in a place of practical understanding in our everyday lives. Money is a huge issue for many people, and that includes those of us in the body of Christ. We really stress giving and tithing, and I do both without hesitation. However, we desperately need to offer more about how to live on a budget and make our financial lives more practical. We tend to make the same uninformed and uneducated guesses with our finances. The more we learn how to handle our daily finances, the more we can give into the kingdom! Now that is something to think about.

If this a stressful part of your life, seek help and

learn how to become more financially savvy. It really doesn't matter if you work at the local fast-food place or Capitol Hill. It is about adjusting your decisions to fit your budget. You can do, save, and utilize more that you currently think you can. There are plenty of books and teachings out there, but if you are like me and have a torrid past with numbers, I recommend a simple format and teaching. I personally used *Financial Peace* by Dave Ramsey.

That gift box I got from my friend that day changed my whole life in that arena. I am grateful for the anointing on that author's life to teach and share with us. You may not be able to apply every teaching you hear, but take what fits, run with it, and don't look back!

Chapter 10

Live Well

And the Lord's servant must not be

quarrelsome but must be kind to everyone,

able to teach, not resentful.

—2 Timothy 2:24 (NIV)

I am so thankful for where I live and the leadership and church family that I have grown to know and love. One of the things I have noticed since being here in Texas is how people live well on purpose. They live with balance in mind. You would have to peek into my background in ministry work to see how this was not always advocated for me. I was not given permission to live well and seek my personal path for my life by those in authority over me in ministry.

I believe in being connected to the local church. It is what the Bible teaches us, and I do not have a problem with it at all. I believe in serving in the local church. I think it is pivotal to growth and maturity in the body of Christ. Serving in your local church will teach you how to hold your tongue and worship God in spite of the cross look or sharp word you just got from Sister Wonderful. The more you see and encounter attitudes, words, and looks you don't like or think are very godly, the more you should be checking yourself and making sure you are an example of Christ.

One of the most irritating and immature responses of anyone attending a church and not serving is complaining. I always say, "Then sign up and show us how to do it perfectly!" The people who have so much to say about Christians don't serve anyone but themselves. I say it nicely—but honestly!

There is an order for how we should structure our lives. God comes first. It is about our personal relationship with Him. Family comes next. "Take care of your household because you are considered worse than an infidel if you don't" (1 Timothy 5:8). Ministry comes third. This is about the calling or purpose of destiny you feel God has given you. Everything else comes after these three things. If one of them is out of order, your life is out of balance—and you are probably feeling the weight of it even as you read these words.

That has not always been stressed in the ministries I have known or been a part of in the past. What was stressed and ingrained in me—more than anything— was the work of the ministry. My dreams, desires, and personal purpose were without merit, and I did not sense that anyone cared! I did many "good" things in ministry, but I am not sure they were all God-directed things for me.

When I moved to Texas ten years ago, I was severely

out of balance. My life was extremely stagnant. I really needed a complete change of scenery, and I hoped my life would become better in so many facets! I was sick and tired of being sick and tired. I was exhausted with the church experience and life. It was so sad in many ways. Unfortunately, many churches open doors on Sunday and practice rote memorization or routine. Many of them have an agenda that is not concerned with our heavenly Father's business. Most people look forward to the Sunday brunches and dinners more than the actual experience at church.

My greatest hope is to impact those I encounter daily. Ladies and gentlemen, you can make an impact wherever you are. You don't have to wait to be invited to Pastor Wonderful's church or be on a Significant Public Figure's television show. You don't even have to hold a certain position or job title. People are drawn to God if you give Him room to work in you. As a result of Him dying on the cross, he will draw people to Himself (John 12:32).

Use the space you take up every day to live the life you proclaim. There are hurting people all around us in need. Pray that the Lord opens your eyes and gives you wisdom. There are hurts in your job, neighborhood, active organizations, grocery stores, churches, and Walmart. I will forewarn you not to go walking into these places with your coffee table Bible trying to lay hands on people, speaking in tongues, and terrifying the heebie-jeebies (a Mississippi word for sure) out of folks! Use wisdom my friend. Let the Word be in you!

If you remain in a place of prayer and maintain a healthy relationship with God, He will use you anywhere. I have been an experiment for it all: Walmart, birthday parties, retreats, sabbaticals, vacations, work (non-Christian setting), the grocery store, and church. Be open and learn to hear the voice of the Lord as He directs you. Just because you have an opinion or know something, it is not always your time to express it openly.

When I connected with my church, I was given a wonderful opportunity to do a mission trip, which I had been deeply interested in doing, but it had never been promoted at my previous church. I became a part of leadership again, but there was so much more balance embedded in what I did. If you have ever worked in ministry, you know it is not easy work. It is a hard-pressed battle in the spiritual realm.

I have not always lived my best life. I have had great experiences and done some things I thoroughly enjoyed, but the amount of stress was unreal—and the focus was terribly off balance. My life was not being lived well in many facets. It was simply rote memorization or making decisions by the seat of my pants. I spent much of my time pleasing those around me and sacrificing my own life and my own desires to "keep the peace" or for the "sake of the ministry" as I was told on many occasions. If it was a sacrifice for the ministry, I felt like it must be a God thing.

I do not hold any grudges. I am not upset in any way about the imbalances of my past. I accept full responsibility for my choices. I am a mature woman in Christ. I must trust that God is able to do so much better than what was accomplished in my past. I have learned so much, and it has helped me become who I am. I am grateful for that. Today, I am simply wiser, and I am more grateful for this time in my life.

If you have experienced any of these experiences or are going through challenging places, I pray for the wisdom of God to overtake you and lead you into the next decision you make. You may not have the option of moving to another city or state as I did, but perhaps you can develop more boundaries to help you live a better quality of life. It is not God's will for you to become despondent and burned out.

How can we effectively minister, serve, and be used

by God when we are exhausted or numb? How can we sufficiently serve others and have a great impact on their lives if we live with offenses? How can we do the work of the kingdom with lasting effects if we don't have perfect love and freedom from unforgiveness or grudges? God wants you to live more excellently in all things. How can we do anything for the church of God if our own households are not in order (1 Timothy 3:5)? That is certainly a question to think about.

If you are sincere about finding more balance in your life, please pray this prayer with me. God knows the concerns of your heart, and He judges the intent of your heart:

All-knowing Father, You are God alone. Forgive me for my sin of pride and omission in the affairs of my life. Today, I put my hope and trust in You to make every crooked place straight. I realize that I am nothing without you. I know You have created me with purpose and ordained destiny for my life.

Forgive me for allowing others to dictate who I am
in You. From this day forward, I will study, learn,
and activate the purpose of which I am called.
I will listen closely for Your voice because Your
Word tells me that Your sheep know Your voice.

I will walk in obedience and love without
reservation. This is what You have commanded
me to do. From this day forward, I will walk
with purpose and destiny in mind. Show me the
path, Abba. Teach me how to speak with grace.
Teach me how to boldly enforce my boundaries
so that I may stay on course with You. Cover
me and protect me as I actively pursue You.

You are God alone, and it is my desire to please
You and make the greatest impact in the area
I am called to attend. Show me how to do that!
Connect me with those who are to support me.

Help me to flee quickly when I encounter dream killers and those who do not believe! I believe, and therefore I speak. Let it be done on earth as it is in heaven! In the name of Jesus, I pray. Amen.

Chapter 11

Connection Matters

A friend loves at all times, and a brother

is born for a time of adversity.

—Proverbs 17:17 (NIV)

There are many things that cause a disturbance in the pit of my stomach, but one for sure is when I hear people say they don't need anyone. Just think about those words for a minute.

I have never met a person in my life who did not need help from another individual at some point in their lives—and neither has my dad in his seventies or my grandmother who lived to be ninety-nine and a half years old. Everyone needs someone at some time. I think we should be saying that we don't need the world at large to show up for our milestones in life, cheer us on in the background, and approve of what we do. This is true. Everyone cannot be there for everything, and in most cases, you do not want them to show up for such events. However, you do need a few good friends.

The very structure of our creation is three parts in one: a body, a soul, and a spirit. When these three parts do not connect with one another, we are in a terrible fix. When the soul is disturbed, the body will feel the effects. When the spirit is low or high, the body will respond to that. When we don't take care of our bodies, we inadvertently experience issues in our souls and spirits. Yes, connection matters. Healthy connections. Being connected well. Yes, you will eventually need someone in some way.

God is made of three persons as well: Father, Son, and Holy Spirit. He fathers us according to our daily needs. He rewards us and corrects us. He gently leads us and guides us. Along the way, He surprises us with simple pleasures and the desires of our hearts. He provides an advocate for us in His Son, Jesus. Jesus is our heavenly attorney. He stands on guard for us and reminds God of how He died for us when we were still doubting who He is, denying Him although He had been actively observed to perform His miracles, execute great teachings to all walks of life, and heal many people.

We also have the person of the Holy Spirit. He is our private cheerleader. He guides us gently in our daily lives if we choose to listen. He stirs our hearts to be kind, giving, and loving. He nudges us to treat others well and make better decisions in our daily lives. The Holy Spirit teaches us how to recognize our worth and know who we are in Him. He guides us in how to live a quality-filled life that honors God and who we say we are in God.

Without that connection to God in all forms of Himself, we would be a complete train wreck. Those who choose to live without Him are mostly likely experiencing life as a series of miniature catastrophes. They depend on education, personal wisdom, and the voices of others. You may be insecure about your future. You may be insecure about the future of your children. I want to remind you that you are never alone—and you need a friend who will be with you even when you don't care to be with Him.

He will hold your hands when they are dirty. He will wash your feet when they have been to unmentionable places. He will feed you even when you have been overlooking the hungry. He will clothe you when you are naked or guilty of mocking those who are. He will put a roof over your head when you have various opinions about the homeless. Do you have a friend like this?

One of the most sobering things I have learned

in my life is that I *do* need people. I am not talking about crowds, fans, or fair-weather people. I am talking about people who would walk ten miles in the snow—uphill. There have been times when I have felt that I would not be able to go on, but lifelong friends, coworkers, and seasonal friends have come alongside me. With their encouragement, I realized that I could do more than I ever thought possible.

I remember when I entered my first and only 10K race. It was an event that my church was sponsoring, and we had the opportunity to raise money for our favorite charity. I have dear friends who rescue children who are trapped in sex trafficking rings as their God-given ministry. I was so excited to raise money for this ministry and get some exercise in the process. That was my dreamy way of looking at it. I planned and worked out to build my endurance before the race. However, when I committed, I did not know that a 10K was 6.2 miles. Bless my heart! I have no idea what I thought it was, but I was sure that I could do it because I power walked about two miles about three times a week. Surely, I could do this! Once I got my facts and numbers straight, I knew I was in for a challenge.

Although I exercised regularly, I was on my own time when I did those power walks. To complete the race in three hours, I would need to build speed and endurance. It was quite a challenge, and I worked through it. On the day of the race, I was mentally ready—or so I thought. I had recently started jogging—at the age of forty—and I thought I would start the race with a light jog! That lasted all of a quarter of a mile. I slowed down to a power walk and got into a rhythm. As I walked, I noticed my pace was getting slower and slower. I was running out of steam by the time I hit the four-mile marker. I thought, *Dear Lord, how much longer?*

By the five-mile marker, I began to sense the finish

line. I only had 1.2 miles to go, but I was exhausted. I remember all the people who had volunteered to be cheerleaders as we made significant milestones along the way. When I was about a quarter mile away from the finish line, I wanted to sit down on the street and cry. I felt like I could not go on. I had nothing left to give.

I was not sure where the timer was, and I was secretly hoping I would not embarrass myself by taking on too much. As I was deciding whether to stay with it or just stop, a dear friend who was serving as a race cheerleader that day mentioned that I was the last one to hit that milestone—and the end was not far now.

She said, "My job as sidewalk cheerleader is over, but I would love to walk with you and accompany you to the finish line if you don't mind."

To this day, she has no idea how timely her intervention was and how God used her to keep me on my feet and focused on crossing the finish line. At that point, I couldn't even talk. I just looked at her and smiled and nodded. I gestured for her to "please walk with me."

What a defining moment! What a time of triumph and jubilation. I laid it all on the line in victory. I crossed that finish line that day with tears streaming down my face and resolve in my heart. I had accomplished victory, and I had one minute to spare before the 10K would be officially over! What a friend I had in Jesus—shining through my personal cheerleader assigned to me that day. Yes, I severely needed someone to encourage me to complete my course!

In life, we cannot predict our times of great need. It goes above needing a warm body. We often need someone who understands and connects *well* and *healthy*. There was no need for conversation as I completed that walk. She simply supported me by just being there. I went into that race very idealistic and confident that I could do it based upon previous workout experiences. I did not anticipate the mental and physical challenge that would accompany that 6.2-mile journey. I am forever grateful to my friend, Shelli, for being used tremendously by God as encouragement and comfort even though she may have been unaware of my needs in that moment.

Chapter 12

In All Things, Be Thankful

We acquire the strength we have overcome.

—Ralph Waldo Emerson

One thing is for certain in this life on earth: we will have troubles. It is insanity to think that anyone has a life of perfection, without difficulty or adversity at some point. One of the most noted things about adversity is that it does not discriminate. It does not care what race, religion, background, socioeconomic status, or position you hold in this life. It is an uninvited guest (mostly), and it plans to visit everyone a few times in life. For this reason, we must strive to gain a different perspective for how to contend with it.

I am not at all immune to the visitation of adversity. I have shared some concerning moments and times of deep adversity. While it may be an unwelcome situation, I believe that the way we contend with this potential intruder will help us rise to a new level of being who we were created to be. Like many of us, I used to heavily ponder why this thing was happening to me. I asked a zillion questions of God.

As I tried to figure it out, I talked to trusted friends and loved ones. Like most of us, I spent countless hours crying, calling out to God—without answers during the moment—and trying to logically figure it out. If you don't know by now, let me inform you that none of these things worked. Don't get me wrong. I know my tears are bottled up in heaven—just as His Word has promised me that they are. I know God is concerned about my thoughts and my needs, and we don't have a high priest who hasn't been touched with our infirmities.

When I was in the thick of going through a deep, dark season in my life, I suddenly had a heart change and a paradigm shift. I had been fighting the fight for a few months, but there was no light at the end of the tunnel. I was sitting in my living room in my queen's chair—my nickname for it since it is huge and extremely sturdy because of the era it was made—having my time with the Lord. As I sat there, I suddenly realized how exhausted I was. It was not from a hard day of work or manual labor, but my exhaustion was from fighting the will of the Lord. I was tired of being frustrated and depleted of motivation. I was tired of asking God to help me without seemingly ever getting any help. I sat in church on Sundays and listened without response because I was struggling to believe because of the darkness around me.

At that point, I simply gave up my current position. There were no more questions, no more demands, and no more chaos in my mind. I just shifted my mind-set to say two words: "thank you." I began to thank God for all the little things and all the big things. I thanked God for all the things I could see and couldn't see. I began to thank Him for His promises. I pulled out my journal and began to write down everything I was thankful for. I filled the next couple of pages. I wrote until I had to stop and think of something else. There is always something else to be grateful for. In that moment, I began to experience a great wave of peace.

My situation was still the same, but the peace that flooded my soul, mind, and spirit could not be measured. I began to breathe it in and seek it every day. I was longing for that special place of peace where I felt safe and loved. I wanted to know that my life mattered to someone as big as God. That was the beginning of the end of my deep, dark tunnel. The days came and passed, and the moments took on a new momentum for me.

I began to see the sunshine instead of the rain

clouds in my life. I began to enjoy smiling naturally instead of it being a forced decision that I was making. I began to thank God for where I was going without dwelling on my current situation. I knew that things had to change; no one could live forever in that state. I began to see a light at the end of the tunnel, and it wasn't the train headed for me. It was the light of a new day. My days were filled with purpose and destiny. My days were filled with divine connections and dreams that were coming alive. It was a day of recompense and renewal. It was a day like none I had seen before.

God did hear my prayers, and He answered them too. It was not on my timetable or how I potentially wanted Him, but it was as He deemed it necessary and in a way I could have never dreamed or orchestrated myself. He opened a great space of increase in my life that could have only come from Him. He covered me with a cloak of favor that serves His kingdom well outside of the four walls of the church.

I learned that adversity can produce a better version of you. However, you must be in a state of mind to keep moving forward and trust God even when you don't understand what He is doing in your life. Giving up is not the answer, and it will dilute your perception in a negative way. I had certainly experienced adversity before, and some things were completely devastating in my world, but this particular space of darkness had no rhyme or reason to it. That went on for months. Of course, like many of you, I sometimes operate like I am smarter than God. I was trying my best to make sense of it all and why it had happened to me. I would rationalize it in my head that I am a faithful tither and attend church regularly. I treat people right—as best as I can—while encapsulating the fruit of kindness. I give to the poor, and I serve at my local church, which ought to earn me at least three jewels in my crown. Let's pause here and lift our hands! However, adversity still found me.

I know I'm not the only Christian who has thought this way. My world was slowly sinking, and I felt helpless and hopeless. I share this so that you don't have to feel badly about it. I asked God to forgive me for those self-righteous thoughts. Even in my perceived best state, I am like filthy rags in His presence.

> But we are all like an unclean thing, And all our righteousness are like filthy rags; We all fade as a leaf, And our iniquities, like the wind, Have taken us away. (Isaiah 64:6 NKJV)

I recently watched a video about an athlete who encountered a horrible accident on the football field. As a result, his left arm was severely damaged. It basically ended his football career before he had the opportunity to be drafted by the NFL. Inky Johnson was eight games away from the NFL draft, and one terrible hit on the field changed that option forever.

Inky never felt sorry for himself or blamed anyone else. Instead, he decided he was going to make it through this terrible moment in life and come out on top. He spoke with such conviction about how every decision we make determines the outcome of our lives tomorrow. While listening to him, I began to thank God for this reminder of how much I had grown by assuming responsibility and taking ownership of my choices. They are not all perfect and filled with wisdom. I have made hasty, tired, low-vision, and angry decisions that have cost me dearly. I take ownership of that, and I lay it at the feet of God. Only He can take my mushy mess and create some semblance of order in it.

I have also made some great, mind-blowing, wisdom-filled, well-thought-out, and Holy Spirit-inspired decisions. Sometimes my choices worked with great results, and sometimes they have broken my heart! Again, I take ownership of those choices and lay them at the feet of our Lord and Savior because only He can produce miracles!

You may have been tempted, fallen for the enemy's voice, or grumbled and complained. You have not taken full responsibility for your actions and blamed your parents, spiritual mentors, friends, or God. Some of you have been through horrible situations and have had adults who were supposed to protect you leave you without covering or meeting your needs. I am heartbroken by stories I have heard over the years and people I have prayed with and for.

If we believe that God is all-powerful, all-knowing, and sovereign in His ways, is there anything He cannot do to make things right in our lives? No matter how much we have been denied, destroyed, and disassembled, He is capable of making it right! Do you really believe He can?

God has commanded us to be thankful in every space of our lives. We are a reflection of Him, His glory, and His abilities. In difficult situations, we have been made victorious through the obedience of Christ. We often forget that we are victorious! When we pause to thank God for the kind and unkind spaces in our lives, it puts us in a position to receive everything He is doing in us to keep us maturing, growing, and attaining level after level of His glory.

I have learned to be thankful through the many highs and lows of my life. I have learned so much in the low and dark places. I have maintained and rejoiced in the good times and the bad times. There have been times when I didn't know how my rent was going to be paid, but I was thankful for the favor of the lady in the front office who handled my account. I remember being thankful for an opportunity for God to bring forth a miracle since I clearly needed one.

A few months after leaving Mississippi—and everything I knew as comfort and security—there was a knock on my door. A man in a mechanic's uniform informed me that he had orders to pick up my car due to lack of payment. It was being repossessed. That was a very dark time in my life.

First of all, these people don't usually knock on your door to let you know these things. They have a mission; therefore, they just hook and take. He wanted to let me know he was taking my car, and he asked me if I would like to get my possessions out of it. He noticed two Bibles on the back seat. I'm not sure if he was terrified of the Word blowing up while he was en route—or if he was a believer who understood hard times and how they find us all. I got my belongings out of my car, walked back into the apartment, sat in the middle of the living room floor, and thanked God for being treated like I mattered during such a stressful time.

Six weeks later, I found myself back in the flow of life. I was thankful for all that God was doing. I was on my way to Atlanta to pick up a car that my favorite uncle had helped me acquire. God was so faithful in that process, and He guided our steps to the car for the right price in that season.

I learned I must guard my mind and thoughts by staying connected to His Word and His promises. For that season and the many challenges that would come, I began to remind God of His Word. There was no argument there. I reminded Him, and I thanked Him for doing it. I thanked Him in advance, and as I thanked Him, my place of peace grew bigger and bigger. I recognized how finite my thought processes, knowledge, and wisdom were compared to what I began to experience and capture through what God was doing. He helped me get back into my space of being his daughter and not His "assistant general" of the universe. I am grateful, and I take pleasure and honor in remaining a daughter. There are days when I struggle with not having control, but I mostly am thankful for God being in control of it all!

Chapter 13

Be Intentional

Life itself is a privilege, but to live life to
the fullest—well, that is a choice.

—Andy Andrews

We live in a time when our attention and our lives
are dominated by the media—if we allow them to
be. So many things in the world are pulling for our
attention. Because the world is literally in the palm
of our hands, we have succumbed to the many open
doors of the media that feed us negatively. During the
recent presidential elections, we discovered there was
"real" news and "fake" news. This—on top of all the

bantering taking place by each of the candidates—was a bit much for me.

We spend countless hours of our precious time scrolling through newsfeeds and pages on social media sites. Unfortunately, we allow what we see to overwhelm us and defeat us. Many of us are experiencing anxiety and depression due to the glamorized lives we think our social media friends are living. We allow a few snapshots of their lives to put us into another state of mind. We feel that we are missing out on life and what it has to offer because they have a monopoly on fun, family, jobs, or money.

I am here to tell you the devil is a liar! You see what people want you to see. Many of these people have struggles just like we all do, but they choose to keep them out of their social media feeds. They have frustrations, family issues, financial problems, job-related issues, and other struggles. However, to keep you out of the loop about the ugly and indifferent parts of their lives, they only post the good, upbeat, happy moments and sentimental milestones. Your perceptions of what you read on these sites are your responsibility.

My saddest moments of browsing social media are when I come across a post where a person has shared too much on the world wide web. They have put themselves in a compromising position or showed a side of themselves that they will more than likely regret once the initial anger or state of mind has worn off. Sometimes when I read such a post, I think, *Wow, they need a friend. They sound desperate for someone to listen or validate them.*

At other times, I think, *Just because you have an opinion does not always mean you need to share it. Just saying!*

When I created my first social media account years ago, I actually did not sign myself up for it. I had a dear friend who was savvier and more technical in all this new wave movement sign me up. I got a lesson on how to check it and how to post, and that was pretty much how I was introduced to it. I was very excited for a few weeks when I connected with old friends from high school and college. It really made the world much smaller, and I felt more connected to people I had genuinely missed and longed to keep in touch with. Family became one of the greatest parts because I could connect with faraway cousins and relatives.

As a professor of communications in the Dallas-Fort Worth area, I keep my theories in practice whether I am teaching or not. I study people's communication even when I am not trying to do so. I study how they communicate even when they do not say a word. Nonverbal communication is more believable than verbal communication. Early on, in this social media game, I noticed that people would post some of the most interestingly inappropriate things. Some of the things were not kind or considerate. Many statements would never be said to someone's face. I have noticed these things from the beginning of my social media experience, and it has only gotten worse.

This social media thing makes me think about how these people act and respond on a daily basis at their jobs, in their homes, with their friends and family, or in times of crisis. For the believers, how many of us respond in a way that would please God? How many of us really show forth what we consistently preach to others when they are ugly and mean to us? Are we pretending? Do we really mean what we say? We attend church on Sunday, but on Monday, no one knows we love Jesus? Do we speak Christian jargon all day long on the job—"Praise the Lord," "Thank you, Jesus," and "I'll pray for you"—but as soon as something goes down that we don't care for, the wrath of God comes through us to the person who offended us!

On people's social media posts, I often saw praises to God, requests for prayers, or public thank yous to

God for doing something they approve of or desire to see done. The next day, this person is cursing out government officials or people who offended them in the past twenty-four hours. However, less than twenty-four hours ago, God was the center of their universe!

The intent of our hearts is often spoken of when we make a mistake, forget to respond in a timely manner, or have been gravely misunderstood. The intentions of our hearts are made aware in times when we feel we need to move into a place of betterment or desire. I looked up several meanings of the word *intention* and found one that resonated with me in Merriam-Webster: "a determination to act a certain way, resolve." This definition talks about being determined to act a certain way—and being resolved in that determination.

In my walk with the Lord over the years, I have had to decide to act or respond in certain ways. There have been many times that I had to resolve to stand strong. I have wrestled with forgiveness of others who have hurt me. I have wrestled with being kind to people who are flat-out rude and inconsiderate. I have wrestled with loving people when they were unloving. I have also wrestled with obedience to God. In all these things, I decided what I knew and know about God. I was determined to do it His way and watch His blessings flow in my life. Therefore, I resolved to do all those things whether I wanted to or not. As I practiced them, God dealt severely with my heart, and it became a more natural response over time.

The scripture that really challenged me when I was in this place was one that we only like to hear when someone else is in the wrong. The scripture holds a more loving correction than we know exactly what to do with:

> For the Word of God is living and active
> and full of power [making it operative,
> energizing, and effective]. It is sharper
> than any two-edged sword, penetrating

as far as the division of the soul and spirit [the completeness of a person], and of both joints and marrow [the deepest parts of our nature], exposing and judging the very thoughts and intentions of the heart. (Hebrews 4:7 AMP)

Reading and getting familiar with this scripture changes your life if you allow it to do so. I am so thankful for how perfect God is in His ways. We spend many days and years of our lives trying to change God to fit us, but He is God!

He expresses in His Word, "I do not change." (Malachi 3:6 NKJV)

When we realize that we are not large and in charge, we can begin to humble ourselves before God and allow Him to do greater work in us than we had been trying to do ourselves. Scripture clearly explains that the Word of God is packed with so much power that it will separate our thoughts and intents! God gives us a way to correct even during our thought processes. We should follow that correction until the end, but many of us ignore it and pray for the best.

I challenge you to be intentional in everything you do. Be kind, loving, compassionate, and caring. Intentionally respond in a way that honors God and pleases Him. Build up the kingdom as much as you possibly can rather than reproaching and tearing it down. Be intentional with how you respond to your family, friends, and loved ones. Open a space in your heart for intention to take up residence. People know genuine and authentic every time. It looks like God, it feels like God, and people will usually respond more favorably to it. Live intentionally. Buy intentionally. Love intentionally. Engage intentionally. Connect intentionally.

My personal experience tells me that living a life of intentionality works better than how I may feel in the moment. It is how I live my life. I like to engage people because I don't know what may be going on behind the scenes in their lives. I like to learn names, call their names, and leave them with some form of compliment that I have noticed in our time of engagement. *Intentional impact* is what I call this measure of communication. I definitely miss the mark here and there, but intention is highly important in my life. I use intentional movements to help me reach my goals. What do you need to intentionally do this year? Who do you need to intentionally connect with? What do you need to intentionally learn this year?

One of the things I admired most about my mother was that she was very particular about the company she kept. My parents were active leaders in the little church I grew up in, and they made sure to teach us how to be good judges of character to the best of their ability. Our church was made up of a few families, and there were about three hundred members. My mother was the church's clerk, and as a child, I was always very inquisitive about everything she did. She used to keep the records in order and make sure new members, baptisms, and salvations were documented. She had very few friends who were her age. In a small town, life is a little different. Everyone has a tendency to peek their noses into everyone else's lives because that is their only source of entertainment.

My mother did not frolic much with people in her age group, but she leaned heavily on a few older women in the community. They had lived good, long lives, and they carried much wisdom. My baby sister's godmother was a golden-aged lady named Ms. Nancy. She had no children of her own, but she wholeheartedly claimed my baby sister like she was her own granddaughter.

Home mission groups were held from house to house, and everyone in the group was a senior citizen besides my mother and maybe two other ladies. Today, we call these groups *small groups*. My mother loved being surrounded by wisdom and authenticity. I could not grasp the reason for her aligned friendships at that time, but I learned to embrace them because of what they had to offer. I often find myself migrating to similar characteristics in people. I do have good friends my age, but I am always intrigued by those who are older than me by more than ten years. I draw from their wisdom. I love the truth and honesty they walk with, and I admire them for their grace. It is really a pleasure to sit with them and listen and glean.

Who you are surrounded by in your life? Who do you trust? Who are you sharing your visions, goals, and dreams with? Are you being mentored by them? The Bible teaches us that iron sharpens iron:

> As iron sharpens iron, so a man sharpens the countenance of his friend. (Proverbs 27:17 NKJV)

I have been so blessed, comforted, corrected, and

redirected as I have forged great relationships with women who were my seniors, my age, and younger. I am at the lovely age where I don't spend much time with anyone or anything that isn't contributing to my life. My goal is to stay in the path of strategic movement. I am walking toward the next level of goals and desires. Everyone who is not a part of that will have to simply read about it. I am always available to be used by God along the way. Intentional Lane is where I am!

As you finish this chapter, make a list of the close friends you spend time with and have intimate conversations with. Are they advancing who you are and who you want to become? Are they supporting you? Are they doubting everything you feel God is telling you to do? Are they helping you create boundaries when you take a wrong turn? Do they pray with you and for you? Are they challenging you with your words, conversations, and connections? Are you learning from them? Are they learning from you?

To live a fully engaged life, we need healthy connections, relationships, and actions on a daily basis. We can conquer so much more together than separately. We also must make sure that our connections help us grow. Growing and maturing in life can bring pain, but healthy growth should be the main focus of our lives. If we choose better, we live better.

Chapter 14

A Time to Love

Love never fails.

—1 Corinthians 13:8 (NIV)

When I was in my late twenties, I experienced a few life-changing moments. I came into my own space around twenty-eight and didn't look back. However, life kept presenting areas of my life that needed attention. I am not the same girl I was once I decided to face north. I also realized that I wanted more for my life. The place and the space I was in did not feed into my dreams and goals. I had so many dreams that I wanted to see fulfilled, but my daily grind caused me to feel helpless and hopeless at times. By that age,

I thought I would be married with at least one child. Unfortunately, there was no husband in sight.

I was teaching at the time, but it wasn't my dream job. In fact, I had just received my undergrad degree a year earlier after taking a break from college. I thought I would be living in another city or state—with my husband—but I was still living in that small college town in Mississippi. So many things were on my heart, and there was not one manifestation in sight. No one else seemed to care. I was just doing life in rote memorization. I decided to invest in myself and move to another space. Once I began to tap into more self-care, self-help, and self-love, life became brand-new. I saw things with a different perspective, and I recognized that people treated me the way I treated myself. No matter what I didn't like or love about my life, all the ugliness and yucky spaces, my decisions played a major role in my outcomes. Change was on the horizon.

The same is true when you deal with the ugly and unlovely in life. I have encountered many friends and acquaintances over the years. On more than one occasion, I have been required to love the unlovely, the backstabber, the liar, and the unfaithful. God has such a great sense of humor. We often cross paths with people who treat us like less than we deserve, and we spend a whole lot of energy trying to figure out why. For ladies reading this book, you may equate this to a former boyfriend or husband. For the men reading this book, you may equate this to a former girlfriend or wife. As for me, I have experienced a couple of relationships when dating that I wondered what I was thinking when it was all over. I have also experienced relationships where I was treated like less than my value.

I have had friends who have baffled me with how much they pushed my limits and boundaries. I have often been surprised by the lack of their boundaries.

I have been betrayed and denied due to other people's lack of self-confidence, and punishment was sent toward me. I have stood tall and brave with people when others thought they were worthless.

A dear friend of mine went through a tough season about two years before she got married. She was desperately trying to break a relationship that was not part of the vision that God had for her life. It was challenging, and she really needed a support system to get through it. On a beautiful sunny day after church, I noticed her standing on the side of the building as people were heading to their cars. She was talking to a few people.

As I passed by, the Holy Spirit said, "Go back and tell her you will fast with her. You will be a support system in her quest for freedom."

I thought, *Okay*. However, I was not sure what I was supposed to be fighting for—or even if I had actually heard God.

I thought, *Is this You, Lord, or the devil?* How often do we do that?

I got out of my car and asked her to step over for a minute. When she came over, I told her what the Holy Spirit had said to me, and she cried right there as we were standing on the edge of the lawn. I told her the Lord said she needed someone to come alongside her and stand with her for the place of deliverance she was seeking. All the directives resonated with her, and we fasted and prayed for a breakthrough in her situation.

Know what God is instructing you to do. Don't follow the crowd—and be careful of others' opinions along the way. I am so thankful that I listened to God and was able to love her through it and other times too. Many of those times have not been favorable moments in her life, but God's love never changed for her. It never changes for us. He takes issue with our behavior. He loves us unconditionally—in the lovely and unlovely times of our lives.

We cannot foresee some of the moments we will encounter, but they will definitely come to us. In college, I experienced a horrible betrayal by a roommate. I discovered a deep issue of deception on her part toward me. It was literally happening before my very eyes, but I had no clue of what had been taking place. I was flabbergasted! I thought, *What did I do to deserve this? Why would God allow this to happen to me?*

That incident had collateral damage in the form of who I saw in the mirror and what I thought of that person looking back at me. I lost a bit of self-esteem during that betrayal and had a bit of ground to recover after that incident. I consulted a mentor on the matter, and she immediately instructed me to fast and pray about the situation. She reminded me that I should keep my heart in the right position with God through it all. I was very hurt and angry when I meditated on it, but I desired healing for my friend and me more than anything.

Today, we are still friends. I had breakfast with her not long ago. It had been years since our last catch-up, but we proceeded without awkwardness. That former situation never came up. I simply attended her in the now and allowed what was then to remain in the past. That is how forgiveness works.

One of the things I have learned over the years is that you cannot force people to like, love, or want to be with you. This is something that has to happen organically. When people are forced to be a part of your life, you will suffer much foolishness and unnecessary conflict as a result. If you don't want to be with me, near me, or around me, you are free to leave. I have learned that loving everyone does not mean we have to be BFFs or eat lunch together on a weekly basis.

It is my choice to be kind, to treat others with respect, and to be wise enough to know how much of a relationship I should pursue with them. It is not always easy to genuinely love people, but it is a requirement from God as one of the greatest commandments Jesus gave us before He departed earth as a human. It also requires leaving judgment at the door. We don't always mean to judge, but we live in a society that promotes it and advertises it through the media. Finding the balance of perspective is one of the most challenging things these days. However, motive will be the crutch of it all.

I have friends who I have had for more than twenty years, and I have gained new friends over the passing years. My intention is to love them all well. I connect with some better than I do with others. There are those who are still full of surprises twenty years later, but I still love them. I only address the things that I feel are impeding me, and I choose my FaceTimes and conversations accordingly. Choice is what I am getting at here. This is how we love the lovely and unlovely well. We review our choices and make wise decisions. No one is forcing us to be friends or to connect with anyone. A coworker who you must deal with several days a week may not be a favorable choice, but you can learn how to love there too.

Sometimes, people seem to come after you for no reason. They show up in your life as you were moving along fine without them, and it seems like they personally want to destroy some part of you. These are the moments when we must seek God diligently and work toward the wisdom of how to overcome and love when we have unlovely actions aimed at us.

My life's mantra includes doing things well no matter how hard it is. One of these things is how I love. There is a way. I may have to dig a little to find a way to do it well, but I will not allow a lack of effort on my part to stop me. Individuals do not have to love me for me to love them with the love of Christ. They do not have to be in my friend circle to be treated with respect and kindness. That should be part of who I am, and I give it to them as a fellow human being:

If it is possible, as much as it depends on
you, live peaceably with all men. (Romans
12:18 NKJV)

Take this time to evaluate and assess your position
about the people in your life. It is too much control
to give over to people when they begin to alter the
person who God intended you to be. It is okay to love
from a distance and pray from afar. God will do the
in-between part. Your assignment is to love well.

Chapter 15

Grit: The Motor of Success

> The only place success comes before
> work is in the dictionary.
> —Vince Lombardi

Grit is firmness of mind or spirit, unyielding courage in the face of hardship or danger

(Merriam-Webster). Some of you may not have heard of this little word that is the support system of success. Grit is defined above, but it is simply the ability and mind-set to keep going when it may seem more logical to give up. My deepest desire for this book is to inspire you in your greatest place of hopelessness. Stand tall even when you stand down. Keep your inside in a good healthy place. In the darkest places of life, I pray that you are inspired deeply. In my darkest places, I allowed the power of the Holy Spirit to operate in me.

You are far greater than what you see in the mirror every day. Your capacity to sustain and endure is inconceivable because the spirit of God is inside you. Your capabilities are greater than you have allowed them to manifest. Dig deeper. Climb higher. Dream larger than life. We serve an incomprehensible God. He alone blew the breath of life into us. The Triune God as a whole is more than our minds can fathom, but the mere fact that He gave us life by blowing His life into us suggests that there is power in us as living beings. When we speak over our lives and imitate what God originally did during our creation, we have the opportunity to watch His promises come to life.

Perhaps you have made terrible mistakes or immature, unwise decisions in your own life. Perhaps you have been rebellious because you wanted things to go your way. God is not holding that against you. He is slow to anger and is filled with mercy. His patience is unfathomable.

> The Lord *is* gracious and full of compassion, Slow to anger and great in mercy. (Psalm 145:8 NKJV)

Perhaps you have made many mistakes in the past. You were not the best daughter, wife, mother, or friend. Perhaps you were not the best son, father, husband, or friend. Maybe your view on how you function as an adult is lacking. God has not given up on you. He has always been there, and He will continue to be there for you. Lean into Him. Ask for the knowledge and wisdom to make better choices and reap better rewards. Be willing to give up your way and try to do things His way. God loves us so much that wisdom is always waiting by the door for us. It is as near as God is, but we must receive it to achieve it.

If any of you lack wisdom, let him ask of God, who gives to all liberally and without reproach, and it will be given to him. (James 1:5 NKJV)

Maybe your failures are a little darker and more secretive. Perhaps you carry envy, jealousy, bitterness, or resentment in your heart. Maybe the more you try to overcome these things, the more you are prompted to think that God does not care about you or the things that concern you. That is an absolute lie from your adversary. God is very concerned about you and the things that concern you.

The Lord will perfect *that which* concerns me; Your mercy, O Lord, *endures* forever; Do not forsake the works of Your hands. (Psalm 138:8 NKJV)

He will also unclutter your heart and put you in a position to be in a better place on the inside. Ask Him to do sol—just like King David did. Ask Him to clean your heart and renew a right spirit in you.

> Create in me a clean heart, O God, And renew a steadfast spirit within me. (Psalm 51:10 NKJV)

Above all, you are not alone. You are not isolated in your events and challenged places in life. The Bible teaches us in Ecclesiastes that there is nothing new under the sun. The enemy desires for you to think that it only happens to you. He desires for you to be consumed with your failures and others' successes. God desires you to recognize that you were never created to walk this path alone. Call on Him! Stand on His Word and remind him of His promises. God will deliver you because He delights in you. Success is in your hands with Him!

He also brought me out into a broad place; He delivered me because He delighted in me. (Psalm 18:19 NKJV)

Because we all have different paths to travel, we will display our grit in different ways. Authors toil over pages and pages of writings, adding and subtracting along the way, until the finished product is just what they feel it needs to be. Athletes take great measures in perfecting their craft and pushing their bodies to the limit and beyond. Entrepreneurs and CEOs make many sacrifices for the sake of their businesses. The employees under them have no clue about the grind and movements that sustain those businesses. Teachers endure various conditions to reach their students and help them discover their aha moments.

When I taught elementary and middle school, I spent much of my own money on supplies that I needed for my classroom. Teachers do not receive the best salaries, and during those times, it was even less. Success does not come without work, and usually the task has a deep element of mundane and sacrificial rotation to it.

Chapter 16

Worship Recklessly

God is Spirit, and those who worship Him
must worship in spirit and truth.

—John 4:24 (NKJV)

One of the habits that I have developed over the years is worshipping the Lord without hesitation. I have learned that God does nothing in convenience, and that includes showing up and prompting the spirit in you to connect with His Spirit. Worshipping Him recklessly has become a way of life for me. I have had encounters in the most interesting places, and I worship him no matter what. Sometimes his anointing, which is His manifested presence in some way, shows up in my kitchen while I am doing the dishes. As I am singing a song, I feel His presence near me. The tears start flowing down my face.

Sometimes, He shows up in my car. As I am riding along and listening to a song, He pops up out of nowhere and overwhelms me with His presence. A divine experience takes place in my car. I sense His presence, I draw near, and I sometimes cry or speak in tongues. I am sure the cars beside me think I am a crazy lady talking to herself.

I often power walk for exercise. As I take a moment to admire all the things He has made, He begins to comfort me. He opens my heart in places that need mending, and He heals the wounds that I have nursed for far too long.

Sometimes He shows up when I am in the shower. I may be overwhelmed by my immediate responsibilities and hating this "adulting" thing. He shows up while I am naked and unashamed, and He assures me that all is well. I respond by shedding the tears that He told us He would bottle up and preserve.

Sometimes He shows up when I am at my job or in a conversation. I remain focused to make sure I honor Him in that moment, and I quietly pray that those who have connected with me in those times will walk away better than when they came to me.

I also aim to worship Him in all I do. I intentionally strive to please Him with the works of my hands and the words of my mouth. I have not perfected this, but my deepest desire is to manifest these characteristics every day of my life.

These are just a few ways that God shows up in my life besides church. He simply communes with me and allows me appointed times to worship Him. For you, the places may depend on your daily routines. If you have not experienced anything like that, you may be wondering how to experience Him in this way.

God is always faithful in trying to connect with

us and love us. It is up to us to make that connection complete. He is a sovereign God, and He can choose to manifest himself in whatever way He wants to do so. We long to be connected to our Creator. We are three-part beings, and our spirits will always gravitate toward the Spirit that created us. We are made in the image of God; therefore, we are created to worship Him. The Bible teaches us that we are made a little lower than angels:

> What is man that You are mindful of him, And the son of man that You visit him? For You have made him a little lower than the angels, And You have crowned him with glory and honor. (Psalm 8:4–5 NKJV)

We return to the truest part of ourselves when we connect with God in worship. All is revealed in His presence, and His love never changes for us. It is true that God does not hate us when we do bad things, but He does hate the bad things we do. Sin causes our separation, and we are connected back to Christ through salvation. Nothing can separate us from that love. Romans 8 gives a clear description of how much God loves us because He will allow nothing to separate us from His love. God tells us that He is married to the backslider. Oh, what magnitude of love!

> "Return, O backsliding children," says
> the Lord; "for I am married to you. I will
> take you, one from a city and two from
> a family, and I will bring you to Zion."
> (Jeremiah 3:14 NKJV)

My challenge to you in this season of your life— whether it is the greatest of times or the darkest of times—is to make room for God. Intentionally plan a time of worship to connect with Him and make room for Him to connect with you. All experiences in life provide opportunities for worship. God is *good*. He is the only one worthy of being called good. He never gives us what we deserve. Many times, it may seem like things are really harsh in our situations, but He is still good! He is *very* good to us!

Be mindful of what you allow into your ears. What you hear is what you repeat and believe. Make sure you are listening to the voices and words that cause you to mature and grow in a healthy relationship with Him. Develop boundaries and open the gates of wisdom. Don't allow just anyone to say anything to you. Be perceptive through the Holy Spirit. Stay connected to the Word of God. It will remind you of who you are and what your promises are from God. He is able to do exceedingly, abundantly, and above all you could ask or think.

Chapter 17

Freedom

So if the Son sets you free, you will be free indeed.

—John 8:36 (NIV)

As I capture what I feel is the last chapter of this book, I've come to a great revelation in my life. I have shared many intimate, heart-wrenching, and embarrassing moments with you, but I am completely at peace with taking ownership of where I may have been a repeat offender or assisted my own capture into hardship.

Sometimes it has been out of ignorance—when I didn't know any other way at the time. Sometimes it has been out of selfishness—when I did not wait for God or I thought I knew a better way. Sometimes it has been the choice of God to allow me to travel that road and experience those things because He counted me as worthy. I struggle with feeling worthy at times—even for God's use and His glory—but I am not the determining agent. God is the one who puts one up and sits another down.

He is the promoter above them all. He is the one who has deemed us worthy before we were born and throughout this journey called life. He sees us worthy and redeemable, but it does come with the balance of correction and love: joyful times and sad times, peace and chaos, mountaintops, valleys, wilderness, sunshine, and rain. The culmination of all these phases of life mature us, grow us, build our character, and cause us to evolve into someone beautiful and in the image of God.

God's love for us never changes. He loved us when we didn't love Him. He has known our potential from the beginning of time, and He chose to give us free will. We are never obligated to love Him or serve Him. If we choose to do so, the benefits go beyond what we could ever know. Romans 8:39 says that "not any other created thing" can separate us from His love. Who would not serve a God like this?

For this reason, I worship Him freely. I am not forced or obligated to do so; I freely choose. I have not personally encountered any other way that brings such wisdom, revelation, and unconditional love. I am free. I am not without problems and issues because that would exclude me from the human race. We are fragile beings, and perfection will not be obtained in these mortal bodies.

It is my sincere hope that the pages of this book have opened a path to you. I pray that the light has brightened and that your heart is available to step into the next space and has evolved into more greatness. Above all, I pray that your faith has been increased and your mind has been renewed, knowing that you are not alone in how you think, feel, and experience. God is with you! He sent me through this book to let you know that you are not without support in the kingdom.

I want to encourage you to do a few things upon finishing this book. Intentionally spend time with God every day. Choose a time that can be uninterrupted time for you. For me, it is morning. It is the first thing I do after waking up. I make my morning smoothie (coffee comes later), go to my little reading nook, and spend time in prayer, reading, and conversation. I have a good friend who is a night owl. She does this at night, and that is fine. The point is to always have designated time with God!

Pray out loud. Set the atmosphere in your home. Speak words out loud into the environment of your home. When people walk in, they will feel the presence of God because of what you have put out there. You can also read scripture out loud.

You are only responsible for your responses. Make sure you are intentional in how you respond. Sometimes it is better to remain quiet than to go back and try to fix our careless words. As my mother used to say, "Choose your battles wisely."

God is good. God is holy. God is faithful!

See beyond the pages of the next book!

April

Citations

Warren, Rick. *https://www.azquotes.com/author/15314-Rick_Warren*, WordPress. https://www.quoteambition.com/.

de Sales, St. Francis. https://aleteia.org/2017/06/01/the-measure-of-love-is-love-without-measure/, WordPress, 2017.

Twain, Mark. rainyquote.com/quotes/mark_twain_106097, WordPress, 2001.

Milne, A. A. https://www.goodreads.com/quotes/6659295-you-are-braver-than-you-believe-stronger-than-you-seem, Goodreads Inc, 2020.

www.biblegateway.com, New King James Version, Thomas Nelson, 1982.

Emerson, Ralph Waldo. https://www.goodreads.com/quotes/6659295, Goodreads, 2020.

Andrews, Andy. https://www.goodreads.com/ quotes/6659295, Goodreads, 2020. https://www. wow4u.com/disappointment-quotes/

Lombardi, Vince. https://www.goodreads.com/ quotes/6659295, Goodreads, 2020.

Printed in the United States
By Bookmasters